PEAK PERFC

CW00693232

MASTERY
OF
YOURSELF

Take The Step Up To
The Next Level

Luther Robbins

Table of Contents

Chapter 1:

To Make Big Gains, Avoid Tiny Losses

Life is a process of adding and subtracting. We add the things that make us better and make life easier. We put aside the things that prove to be a pebble in the shoe.

There is a flaw in human effort and our concept for success. We think that we can achieve more if we focus harder on getting better. We think that if we are not getting worse, we are on the right track. But I can assure you, we are heavily mistaken.

The more we focus on bigger gains, the more we overlook the small things we stop caring about. We give up on relations, hobbies, ethics, love, and the million other losses that we don't measure on the same scale.

We can achieve the same amount of things, the same scale of success, and still, be the better person that we want to be. But we don't need to not work on the smaller details of this successful journey.

Let's say you have achieved it all and now you look back a decade or two. Do you think you won't regret the things that could have been saved in this whole process? But you chose not to or didn't care enough for them, and now you are rich in the pocket but poor in every other sense.

They say money can buy you anything, but it can never buy you happiness. You can have all the money in the world but you can't make sure if you won't ever have any regret.

We all are a creator. We make things, sometimes for ourselves and sometimes for people around us. Sometimes we make things better for us that then prove to be good for someone else as well. But also do things in a way that doesn't affect anyone else in a bad way. At least not deliberately.

Bad things happen, but most of the time we are the reason for them to happen in the first place. We are so devoted to the greater good that we neglect the small things we lose in the process.

Check it with yourself, if you are so devoted to being a better person than you were yesterday, and you have achieved more than yesterday. Then why do you still repeat the small mistakes and take the small losses?

You have to understand the concept of losses over gains. If you invest some money into something, and you are at a small loss every other day, then you can't justify the big profits you might gain some days later.

It is the constant concern to keep away from the small misfortunes or mistakes that might leave you into yet another breakdown. If you truly want to be a free and successful person, you need to have confidence in whatever you do will certainly give you more and more and it won't come at the cost of a single thing.

Take the mantra, reduce your losses and your gains will gain volumes in no time.

Chapter 2:

Stop Being a Slave To Old Beliefs

Life has a beginning for everyone. Everyone has a different life. Everyone has a different belief. Everyone has different brains and different observations. You are that everyone. You are different in every aspect possible except the fact that you are only human life to a billion others.

We humans, as a species have lived history through a certain set of rules. Modern and civilized cultures live with some social decorum and follow some societal beliefs and rituals. But who imposed these laws on us?

Who made these rituals so important for everyone, as if we cannot survive without them? There is no justification for most of these beliefs that are still being practiced to date.

Humans have also the same ways of adapting to thins like other animals. They tend to repeat things to perfect or learn them.

We have practiced so many pointless beliefs and conditions for so long that we are unwilling and unable to even try to think aside them.

We are so scared to look around these beliefs and shake things up a bit to create newer and better outcomes for us and others. But we still feel liable and a slave to this tendency to follow whatever is being imposed on us. No!

You are a free soul. You were born a free soul. You were given a unique mind and you should act like you still have one. You can think of bigger and better ways to make your life easier and more meaningful.

Look at a bird. They start taking lessons from other birds, but when they are finally in the air for the first time, they are now free to do anything they can ever wish to do.

You are also a free bird. You have everything you want to create new beliefs of your own where you don't have to justify or answer to anyone because now you have a person to fall back on. And that person is You!

What if you started a cult today, and someone came and asked you to justify it. Do you think you owe that person an answer? I don't think so!

Because you are a free individual who can anything he or she wants, only if it doesn't hurt anyone else around you.

You started your life alone and you will die alone. So why not live it alone too. I am not saying to give up on all relations. But you should make up your own beliefs if you are not OK with the previous ones.

Don't argue! You cannot force your opinion on anyone else, just like you are not obligated to follow anyone else's.

So from this day in your life. Make a vow to yourself, that you will take every day of your life as if it were a new life and you will discover newer things this time. This will help you find a newer purpose and will eventually create a new ambition for others to follow.

Chapter 3:

6 Ways To Achieve Peak Performance

To be successful requires much more than just your intelligence and talent. There are basic needs which have to be met to function at your peak. These basic needs are neglected by most, impairing their capacity to rise to those elusive higher levels of success and happiness in life.

1. Get enough sleep

Sleep deprivation means peak performance deprivation. Without proper sleep you wake up to meet the day feeling scatterbrained, foggy and unfocused. You grab your cup of coffee to get a charge on your brain, which completely depletes your brain function over the course of the day, making your brain even more exhausted.

Good sleep improves your ability to be patient, retain information, think clearly, make good decisions and be present and alert in all your daily interactions. Sleep is your time off from problem solving.

When you get the proper rest your brain becomes awake, alive and ready to generate the cognitive prowess and emotional regulation you need to function at your peak performance.

2. Drink lemon water

Lemon water is a great substitute for your morning coffee. Although lemons do not contain caffeine, lemon water has excellent pick-me-up properties without negative side effects. It energizes the brain, especially if it is warm, and hydrates your lymph system.

Among the most important benefits of lemon water are its strong antibacterial, antiviral, and immune-boosting power, making sick days from work nearly non-existent. Lemon water cures headache, freshens breath, cleanses the skin, improves digestion, eliminates PMS with its diuretic properties and reduces the acidity in the body.

Most importantly, lemon water increases your cognitive capacity and improves mood with its stimulating properties on the brain, helping you to operate more consistently in your peak performance zone.

3. Get daily exercise

Exercise is the best way to reduce the stress that impairs your performance stamina. Exercise increases your "happy" mood chemicals through the release of endorphins. Endorphins help rid your mind and body of tension alleviating anxiety helping you to calm down.

The brain needs physical activity to stay flexible. Exercise stimulates neurogenesis, or the growth of new brain cells, which improves overall brain function. The development of new brain cells keeps your brain young and in shape, allowing you to be more efficient, pliable and clear in your decision making, higher thinking and learning capacities. Neurogenesis is the catalyst to peak performance.

Further, there is nothing that can bring down self-esteem quicker than not liking how you look. Exercise improves self-confidence and your perception of your attractiveness and self-worth. This confidence contributes greatly to your success, prompting people to respect you and take you seriously

4. Have emotional support

Having healthy, loving relationships increases your happiness, success and longevity by promoting your capacity to function in life as your best self. Social connectedness and love gives you relationships to be motivated for and people to be inspired by.

A strong social network decreases stress, provides you with a sense of belonging and gives your life the deeper meaning it needs. When you are loved and loving, and carving out quality time to cultivate these relationships, you are exalted, elevated and encouraged to live your dreams fully.

5. Be unapologetically optimistic

A requirement of peak performance is to look for the best in every situation. Optimism is the commitment to believe, expect and trust that things in life are rigged in your favor. Even when something bad happens, you find the silver lining.

A positive outlook on life strengthens your immune system and the emotional quality of your life experiences, allowing you to be resilient in the face of fear, stress and challenge.

Being an optimist or a pessimist boils down to the way you talk to yourself. When you are optimistic you are fierce in the belief it is your own actions which result in positive things happening. You live by positive affirmation, take responsibility for your own happiness and anticipate more good things will happen for you in the future. When bad things happen you do not blame yourself, you are simply willing to change yourself.

6. Have time alone

Time alone is refueling to your physical, mental, emotional and spiritual self. This time recharges you, helping to cultivate your peak performance levels again and again. You must give yourself time to recover from the stress of consistently being around others. Being around people continuously wears down your ability to regulate your emotional state, causing self-regulation fatigue. For this reason you must give yourself permission to take the pressure off and disconnect.

Chapter 4:

10 Habits Holding You Back The Power Of Habits

Habits are powerful actions that have become part of our routine. They control our behavior and they determine our progress in life. Our success or failure is a culmination of our habits. Be careful what you adapt lest you regret it.

The habits we develop could either propel us to success or hold us back from achieving our dreams. Here is an insight into ten habits holding you back:

1. Idleness

Idling is not resting. It is staying aimlessly without doing anything. You cannot afford to idle around in the modern world where time is essential in doing business. Time waits for no one. It does not care whether or not you have an emergency, or whether or not you are disadvantaged in any way. The clock will continue ticking and you have to catch up with it.

Idling does not have to be illegal for you to shun it. Always find something to occupy your mind and you will comfortably keep evil thoughts at bay.

2. Assumptions

Assuming everything at face value has killed many dreams. Seek clarification on what is unclear. Life has no grey areas; it is all in black and white. Assumptions create conflicts because of different expectations from both parties.

Conflicts will hold you back because you will have to spend a lot of time resolving them instead of pursuing your dreams. They misplace your priorities in life.

3. Anger

It is an extremely strong emotion that can wreak havoc in your life to your disbelief. Anger is not entirely bad when properly managed. It is a powerful motivator of doing things that would otherwise appear impossible.

Some doors have been shut to your face because you were probably unable to control your anger. Manage your public display of emotions and you will overcome anger.

4. Misinformation

Wisdom is making decisions from a point of knowledge. Ignorance is responsible for a majority of the bad decisions that people make. When you successfully win the battle against ignorance, you will succeed where your predecessors failed.

Unless you eat the humble pie and revisit decisions made in ignorance, you will face the consequences of misinformed decisions. Acquaint yourself with what happens around you lest you regret it later. Knowledge is the weapon to fight ignorance.

5. Getting Stuck In The Past

The past has imprisoned many people and stagnated their progress in life. Everyone has made mistakes they are not proud of and would gladly write them off when given the opportunity. We may be condemned for our past mistakes but that does not define us.

Quit judging yourself on the scale of your past achievements. The present has different challenges to be handled differently and getting stuck in the past is a hindrance to your success.

6. Disconnect With The Future

What is holding you back could be your cluelessness about the future. It is the inevitable fate that everybody will face. Walking into it unarmed with skills on how to survive could hold you back from achieving your goals.

The earlier you connect your mind with the future and the trajectory you want your life to take, the better your chances at making it in life. Plan for the future lest you fail to realize your dreams.

7. Burning Bridges And Building Walls

Healthy relationships are the pillars upon which our lives are built upon. Do not carelessly sever ties with people because you could unknowingly block your destiny connectors.

Be slow to build walls with people or collapse bridges after you have used them because you never know when you will need to use them again. Do not allow unhealthy relationships to hold you back from realizing your dreams.

8. Toxicity

Poison can kill regardless of the quantity it is consumed. Toxicity can poison your dreams and kill the potential within you if it is not curbed on time. What could be holding you back is the baggage you carry around instead of renewing your mindset to face new challenges.

Make a purposeful change of heart to unchain yourself from the shackles of mental captivity. It could derail your progress or kill your dreams altogether.

9. Bad Company

The only cure to a bad company is shunning it and finding a new one that will bring out the best in you. The clique of friends you keep could push you towards your goals or hold you back from achieving your dreams.

You need fresh positive voices around you to preach hope and push you towards success. The power of a good company counters the negative one that holds you back.

10. Imitating Other People

The major hurdle to the youth is imitating other people's lifestyles. It makes you blind to the potential in you and you live a lie until the day you will live an authentic life.

Even though you have mentors you emulate, cut your cloth according to your size. A fake lifestyle will make you live an illusion that will prevent you from advancing in life.

In conclusion, these ten habits will hold you back from attaining the milestones you have set. Carefully work your way around them.

Chapter 5:

10 Habits You Must Stop If You Want

To Manifest What You Want In Life

All of us have dreams that we would like to fulfill. What joy would it be to check our bucket list of wishes! However, there are obstacles on our way that could block the manifestation of our dreams. Here are ten habits that you must stop if you want to manifest what you want in life:

1. Lateness

A lot of people are struggling with timekeeping. What is even sadder is that we are normalizing lateness. Punctuality should be inculcated in our culture for the upcoming generations to understand the significance of observing time.People lose lifetime opportunities to the lateness in job interviews, business meetings, and client deadlines. Lateness demeans your character and casts you as unreliable before the clients and prospective employers.

2. Laziness

Laziness is a threat to personal and business growth. It is often disguised as selective participation but it does not alter what it truly is. It has stagnated the dreams of many people because they were unwilling to go the extra mile.You cannot manifest your desires when you are lazy to pursue them. Manifestation requires hard work and aggressiveness. Do not be lazy to follow your passion and your efforts shall be rewarded.

3. Addiction

Addiction is being excessively used to something that you cannot do without. Although many people consider it normal, it is not one. It is the conditioning of the mind that you cannot perform in the absence of something else.

Addiction to anything can rob you of your breakthrough in life. It makes you a slave to the substance you are addicted to. Blue screen addiction or addiction to drugs or a close friend ties your progress to them. Fight it off to manifest your dreams.

4. Gambling

You can never gamble your way to wealth. Gambling is very addictive because it programs you to think that you cannot achieve anything unless you gamble. You can lose your possessions to gambling if you do not cut off this bad habit on time. As disastrous as gambling is, those affected may need external help to help them overcome it.

5. Wishful Thinking

It is good to have dreams about the future and the direction you would like to steer your life to. However, do not waste all your time in wishful thinking instead of actualizing your dreams. Building castles in the air should have a limit that is not crossed. Work on your vision for you to actualize it. No amount of wishful thinking will bring you closer to your dreams.

6. Jealousy

It is the root of most social problems. There is no need to be envious of other people's achievements. They worked hard to attain their current status and so should you instead of not wishing them well.

Learn to clap for others until your turn reaches. Celebrate their achievements and yours shall be celebrated too. Drop your jealous attitude because it will block others from celebrating you.

7. Keeping Bad Company

You should not keep any bad or negative company because they will influence you to be like them. Be mindful of the people you spend time with. They can sink your ambitions in hopelessness.

To manifest what you want, surround yourself with like-minded people who will support you. They relate to your dreams and can counsel you.

8. Negativity

Negativity has been silently killing the dreams of many people. You may have a viable dream that can be actualized with a little support but when you introduce negativity, it will only remain a dream. Manifestation requires positive confession and attitude. You need to believe that it can be done for you to achieve it. Even though everyone may doubt you, do not doubt yourself. Believe in yourself.

9. Fake Lifestyle

There is a thin line between a fake lifestyle and living your dream. The distinction between them is clearer when you consider the motive. The motive for a fake lifestyle is showing off while living your dream is genuine. Do not for anything else trade your dreams for a fake lifestyle. You will comfortably live within your means as you work for higher glory.

10. Blind Faith

It is most common between political leaders and their followers. Supporters of a political figure are often rubber stamps of what their leaders subscribe to. This is an unhealthy relationship because they blindly follow their leader even at the brink of perishing. You must stop blind faith in men for you to manifest your desires because people can disappoint you. You will get heartbroken and possibly abandon your dreams.

In conclusion, these ten habits have caused many people to stumble and fall never to recover soon enough to regain their crown of glory. Avoid them if you want to be successful.

Chapter 6:

20 Positive Affirmations For Men

A positive affirmation is a statement about yourself that is phrased in the positive, present tense. It reflects an area of your life, emotions, or belief system that you want to improve or change. The potential benefits of affirmations are vast. Positive affirmations empower you to become the best version of yourself. They inspire you to act in ways that help you fulfill your potential. You can use positive affirmations to reprogram negative thoughts into positive beliefs. The ability to reprogram your beliefs about yourself has the potential to transform your life completely.

For an affirmation to be effective, it needs to meet four criteria.

Each positive affirmation you use should be:

1. **Worded in the present tense**
2. **Positive**
3. **Specific**
4. **Personal**

You can create your own positive affirmations using this four-step framework. The benefits of affirmations are dramatically increased when you have created it yourself from an existing negative belief. Let's say you had a belief that you are unsuccessful in your job.

Where focus goes, energy flows. If you keep feeding this belief, it will manifest as truth.

When you understand this, you can see how our thoughts really do shape our reality.Instead, you can use this belief as an opportunity to grow. Take that statement and switch it to its positive opposite. Rather than thinking: 'I am terrible at my job, I'll never get a promotion, my boss hates me,' you now think 'I am great at my job, I love what I do, and I always put 100% effort into every task

Whether you choose to formulate your own positive affirmations or use the ones I have created for you below, you must cultivate a daily practice. The best times to practice are first thing in the morning and last thing at night (or whenever you feel that you need to repeat them to start feeling better). During these times, your mind is more open and will absorb the statements on a deeper level.

It is best if you say them out loud while looking in the mirror. Speaking them to yourself affirms that you trust in yourself, and you believe the statements to be true. If speaking them out loud is not possible, you can say them in your mind. Writing them out a few times a week is also beneficial. Try getting a journal specifically for this purpose. Another technique that you might find useful is to pin the written affirmations to the mirror or refrigerator, where you will see them often.

When you are just beginning with this practice, it may be easy to forget, so set an alert on your phone or in your calendar to remind you. Here are 20 examples of positive affirmations relating to different areas of life.

Choose the ones that resonate most with you.Once you feel that you have integrated those particular statements, you can select or create new ones for other areas you want to improve.

Confidence and Self-Esteem

1: "I feel confident in every situation."

2: "I like who I am."

3: "I am a good person."

4: "I am great at helping people."

5: "I feel valued by my friends and family."

Inner Strength and Resilience

1: "I meet each new challenge with enthusiasm."

2: "I am strong and stable."

3: "I think I can, so I can."

4: "No matter what happens, I can handle it."

5: "I am powerful."

Positivity and Joy

1: **"I radiate joy to everyone I meet."**

2: **"I see the best in people."**

3: **"In the present moment there are no issues, only peace."**

4: **"Happiness is a choice; today, I choose to be happy."**

5: **"I have the power to turn negative thoughts into positive beliefs."**

Career and Success

1: **"I deserve success."**

2: **"I can succeed at whatever I choose."**

3: **"I am good at my job, and I love what I do."**

4: **"I have great ideas."**

5: **"I am innovative and tenacious."**

I hope that my guide to positive affirmations for men has provided you with a solid foundation for designing your perfect practice. Remember, to reap the benefits of affirmations, you should say them out loud every day and write them out a few times a week. Use any of my examples of positive affirmations, or for extra power, try creating your own using my framework. If you commit to a daily practice, you will soon notice the benefits in your career, relationships, emotional resilience, sense of self-worth, and confidence.

Chapter 7:

The 5 Second Rule

Today I'm going to share with you a very special rule in life that has worked wonders for me ever since I discovered it. And that is known as the 5 second rule by Mel Robbins.

You see, on a daily basis, I struggle with motivation and getting things done. I struggle with the littlest things like replying an email, to responding to a work request. This struggle has become such a bad habit that before I think about beginning any sort of work, I would first turn on my Netflix account to watch an episode or two of my favourite sitcom, telling myself that I will get right on it after I satisfy this side of me first.

This habit of procrastination soon became so severe that I would actually sit and end up wasting 4-5 hours of time every morning before I would actually even begin on any work-related stuff. Before I knew it, it would be 3pm and I haven't gotten a single thing done. All the while I was staring at the clock, counting the number of hours I have wasted, while simultaneously addicted to procrastinating that I just could not for the life of me get myself off the couch onto my desk to begin any meaningful work.

I realized that something had to change. If I kept this up, I would not only not get anything done, like ever, but i would also begin to loathe myself for being so incredibly unproductive and useless. This process of self-loathing got worse everyday I leaned into the habit of procrastination. It was only until i stumbled onto Mel Robbin's 5 second rule that I started to see a real change in my habits.

The rule is simple, to count backwards from 5 and to just get up and go do that thing. It sounded stupid to me at first, but it worked. Instead of laying around in bed every morning checking my phone before I woke up, I would count backwards from 5 and as soon as it hit 1, i would get up and head straight towards the shower, or I would pack up my things and get out of my house.

I had identified that staying at home was the one factor that made me the most unproductive person on the planet, and that the only way I knew I was going to get real work done, was to get out of the house. I had also identified that showering was a good way to cleanse my mind from the night before. I really enjoyed showering as I always seem to have a clear head afterwards to be able to focus. What works for me, may not necessarily work for you. You have to identify for yourself when are the times you are most productive, and simply replicate it. A good way to find out is by journaling, which I will talk about in a separate video. Journaling is a good way to capture a moment in time and a particular state of mind. Try it for yourself the next time you are incredibly focused, write down how you got to that state, and simply do it again the next time to get there.

The 5 second rule is so simple yet so powerful because it snaps our unhealthy thought patterns. As Mel puts it, our brain is hardwired to protect us. We procrastinate out of fear of doing the things that are hard, so we have to beat our brain to it by disrupting it first. When we decide to move and take action after reaching 1, it is too late for our brains to stop us. And we get the ball rolling.

I was at my most productive on days that I felt my worst. But I overcame it because I didn't let my brain stop me from myself. I wouldn't say that I am struggle free now, but i knew i had a tool that would work most of the time to get me out of procrastination and into doing some serious work that would move my life forward. There are times when I would forget about the 5 second rule and my bad habits would kick in, but I always reminded myself that it was available to me if I chose to use it.

I would urge all of you who are struggling with any form of procrastination or laziness to give the 5 second rule a try. All you need to do is to get started and the rest becomes easy.

Chapter 8:

Why You Are Setting The Wrong Goals

Ever wondered why you are not getting any closer to your goals? Why you keep failing despite having all that effort? Why does someone else seem to be more successful?

Here are some thoughts for you to ponder.

You may have a good set of skills and all the eligibility criteria anyone else has. But you are not yet in the same spot you wished some years ago. Maybe it is not happening for your right now, because your approach to those goals is not correct. Or, maybe your goals are wrong altogether.

Let's say you had a goal to be someone or achieve something someday. But you never had any idea how to! So you started asking why am I not getting the success that I deserve, but never asked yourself, how can I get to that success.

So you might think that you have the right goals to achieve something. But the reality is, that you never had the right goals.

You should have set a single goal a single day. A single goal that you can achieve in a day will help you get on the right train at the right time with a limited effort.

You shouldn't think of the future itself, but the goal that you might achieve someday. Once you have that goal in mind, you shouldn't need a constant reminder every day just to create a scenario of depression and restlessness that won't help you rather strain unnecessary energy.

Once you have the final goal, put it aside and work towards the small goals that you can achieve in real-time with actual small efforts.

Once you have a grasp of these goals, you will find the next goal yourself; a goal that you might have never thought of before.

Just say you want to lose weight and you want to get to your ideal BMI someday. This is a valid and reasonable Goal to achieve. This might prolong your life and increase your self-worth. So you should have a set of regular goals that ultimately lead you to the final goal.

So you want to lose weight, start by reducing fats and carbs in your next meal, and the one after that and the next one.

It will be hard the first time. Maybe the same at the second time. But when you have envisioned the ultimate goal, you will be content with the healthier alternates as well.

Add 5 minutes of exercise the next day, along with the goals of the previous day. You will be reluctant to do it the first time, but when you see the sweat dripping from your chin, you will see your healthier self in each drop.

Every goal has its process. No matter how much you avoid the process, you will always find yourself at the mercy of mother nature, and nature has always a plan for execution.

Now it's your decision whether to be a part of that process or go down in history with a blank face with no name.

You will always find a way to cheat, but to cheat is another ten steps away from your penultimate goal.

Make it your goal to resist every temptation that makes your day no different than the previous one. Live your life on One day, Monday, Change day principle and you will always find yourself closer to your salvation.

The process of change is mundane. In fact, the process of everything in life is mundane. You have to apply certain steps and procedures for even doing the most basic tasks in your daily life.

Stop procrastinating because you are not fooling anyone else, just yourself. And if you keep fooling yourself, you will be the worst failure in the books of history.

Chapter 9:

10 Habits of Charles Koch

When the name "Charles Koch" and Koch Industries pop up, you most likely have a certain reaction. You may admire Charles as a tugging businessman who built a tiny inherited company into a billion-dollar empire or as a demagogue who uses his fortune to push free-market legislative changes. Rather than focusing on his political side of view, let's focus on his spectacular performance leading his company to such massive success.

Charles Koch is the CEO of Koch Industries, one of the largest privately-owned companies in the United States. The company under his control has amassed dramatic, long-term growth in light of countless other competitors that failed to adapt and cease to exist. So what are his success secrets?

Here are 10 habits of Charles Koch.

1. His Market-Based Philosophy

Charles Koch's book "Good Profit" details his management philosophy, which he calls Market-Based Management (MBM). Instead of focusing on maximizing profits first, Koch insists on a customer-oriented approach to success, which means that your priority is to create value for customers than their alternatives, coupled with the idea of infinity.

2. Apply the Principle of Human Progress

Applying the principle of human progress means believing in yourself and the sustainability of your idea. Believing that your idea will last forever, and also believing in other people. According to Koch, you cannot be doing it all; you need a partner! Most of all, believing in their abilities, empowering them from a bottom-up perspective, bearing in mind that no one is good at everything, and a partner who compliments your capabilities.

3. Knowledge Is Power

Charles is a big fan of reading scientific pieces because he understands the transformative nature of knowledge. Through knowledge, you're able to master several skills and the science of utilizing them to create value. To improve your performance, seek knowledge from all sources that compliment your line of business and share the knowledge proactively while welcoming the challenges.

4. Culture

Critical to performance is an organizational culture that creates room for your business to thrive. Koch's culture is based on behavioral aspects rather than competency, such that he insists on focus, persistence, and discipline to earn superior results. Central to a successful are accountability, leadership, and innovation.

5. Humility and Self-Assuredness

Charles Koch learned the value of hard work, humility, integrity, and long-term dedication from his late father, which he exemplified as core to successful company culture and leadership. He advises against complacency because it's from this that arrogance might be developed. Just as Koch, all you need is to exemplify humility and intellectual honesty as vital to your culture, as arrogance, or complacency are sure prescriptions for business failure.

6. Take Risks and Accept Failure

Perfection is an enemy to innovation, growth, and subsequent profitability. Failure, on the other hand, as Koch observed, is success in progress. Koch's approach to growth is that of a trial and error process. Therefore, the key to the long-term success of your business is your willingness to accept mistakes while treating failure as an opportunity rather than an impediment and mitigating your losses promptly.

7. Challenge and Test Ideas

According to Koch, a business with good ideas and poor execution will ultimately fail. Encouraging the generation of new ideas is a way of innovating and progressing. Hence you need to accommodate and challenge those ideas rather than damagingly criticize them. Allowing the generation of new ideas and information requires creating a culture of free speech, respect, and trust where your employees can share, seek knowledge, solve problems.

8. Empower, Value, and Trust Your People

People are the greatest asset in an organization, which is why within Koch's Guiding Principles, allowing people to learn new techniques leads to innovation. Whatever your position in the organization, you should actively pursue knowledge and substitute viewpoints. Suppose the goal is to create a culture that will be competitive in the long run. In that case, a company must give its employees the appropriate degree of responsibility to achieve a better state.

9. Proper Incentive Programs

According to Koch, employees at his company are rewarded for the value they are expected to create rather than for their positions or roles. Your goal is to motivate the employees to contribute to the greatest extent possible regardless of role.

10. Innovation

If you haven't mastered an innovative culture, your days are numbered! Koch emphasizes the importance of constantly creating innovative products, services and replacing old ones with newer and better ones. Koch industries have progressed and grown due to defining and acquiring businesses that benefit both customers and Koch as a whole.

Conclusion

Koch's success is an ideal example of well-executed ideas, values, and great investing. Many businesses fail to attain their potential or fail because they are afraid of change and prefer hierarchy, structure, and regulations for security and comfort's sake. If Koch and the Investment Masters can do it, shouldn't the businesses you own do the same?

Chapter 10:

When It Is Time To Slow Down

Go faster. Do more. Hustle. Hustle even more. Sound familiar? Social media is full of influencers, entrepreneurs, and "gurus" touting the virtues of hustling at all costs. It's reached the point where hustling, and even just talking about hustling, appears to be more important that actually producing results. People confuse "hustling" with "productivity" and mistake "working" for "results." They don't have a mindfulness practice. They didn't make time for trips, fun, friends, or family. They think that if they worked harder, and worked more hours, they'd be more successful. That is not true if all you do is work, work work. You will be burnt out.

The antidote to the "always hustling" mindset is "slowness." It sounds crazy, but slowing down can be the difference between success or failure, or between thriving and burning out. While more and more personal coaches and social-media influencers, qualified or not, tout the hustle lifestyle, successful leaders and entrepreneurs who actually create results in their lives know that slowing down builds the foundation for their success. Here are four reasons why slowing down can actually help you accelerate your success, enjoy a deeper sense of fulfillment, and create the life you want.

1. What's the point of hustling if you're going in the wrong direction? Too many people work tirelessly down a path that won't give them the results they want. It's like running on a

treadmill...you're working, but you're not going anywhere. Slow down and make time for clarity. You can't see where you're going if you're too busy running with your head down.

2. If your goal is to succeed, then you should be willing to take the time to honor what your mind, body, and spirit need to stay healthy. When every day provides 24 hours, there's really no excuse not to meditate, exercise, cook a healthy meal, or journal.

3. Too many people fail to see the benefits in their emotions. Emotions are a guide, and they help you take inventory of what's happening in and around you, and how best to respond. Successful people feel and manage their emotions, and they don't let them trigger bad behaviors or actions. There's a mantra that sums this up well: If you can name it, you can tame it. By slowing down, you can feel the emotions you're experiencing and describe them. In doing so, you can process them and let them guide you to a healthy response.

4. What good is hustling all the time if a single decision can undo all the work you invested? To put it simply, your mind is like a car engine: If you always have your pedal to the floor, the engine will redline, overheat, and fail. When you slow down and make

time for rest and meditation, you lower your baseline for mental stress. When your mind isn't racing, it's free to absorb information, assess the circumstances, and make a good decision. If success requires making good decisions, and slowing down helps you make better decisions, then consider how you can invest more time in slowing down.

Consider the benefits described above and identify one simple step toward bringing more slowness into your life. See how that goes, and then try more. As someone who hustled himself into a concussion and changed, I can tell you that life is much better when you balance the hustle with slowness.

Chapter 11:

Why You Are Amazing

When was the last time you told yourself that you were amazing? Was it last week, last month, last year, or maybe not even once in your life?

As humans, we always seek to gain validation from our peers. We wait to see if something that we did recently warranted praise or commendation. Either from our colleagues, our bosses, our friends, or even our families. And when we don't receive those words that we expect them to, we think that we are unworthy, or that our work just wasn't good enough. That we are lousy and under serving of praise.

With social media and the power of the internet, these feelings have been amplified. For those of us that look at the likes on our Instagram posts or stories, or the number of followers on Tiktok, Facebook, or Snapchat, we allow ourselves to be subjected to the validation of external forces in order to qualify our self-worth. Whether these are strangers who don't know you at all, or whoever they might be, their approval seems to matter the most to us rather than the approval we can choose to give ourselves.

We believe that we always have to up our game in order to seek happiness. Everytime we don't get the likes, we let it affect our mood for the rest of the day or even the week.

Have you ever thought of how wonderful it is if you are your best cheerleader in life? If the only validation you needed to seek was from yourself? That you were proud of the work you put out there, even if the world disagrees, because you know that you have put your heart and soul into the project and that there was nothing else you could have done better in that moment when you were producing that thing?

I am here to tell you that you are amazing because only you have the power to choose to love yourself unconditionally. You have the power to tell yourself that you are amazing. and that you have the power to look into yourself and be proud of how far you came in life. To be amazed by the things that you have done up until this point, things that other people might not have seen, acknowledged, or given credit to you for. But you can give that credit to yourself. To pat yourself on the back and say "I did a great job".

I believe that we all have this ability to look inwards. That we don't need external forces to tell us we are amazing because deep down, we already know we are.

If nobody else in the world loves you, know that I do. I love your courage, your bravery, your resilience, your heart, your soul, your commitment, and your dedication to live out your best life on this earth. Tell yourself each and everyday that you deserve to be loved, and that you are loved.

Go through life fiercely knowing that you don't need to seek happiness, validations, and approval from others. That you have it inside you all along and that is all you need to keep going.

Chapter 12:

10 Habits For Good Health

Good health is great wealth that we can be proud of. It cannot be equated with any amount of possessions. We follow the doctors' instructions to the latter when we fall sick because we want to regain back our good health. Here are ten habits for good health:

1. Eating A Balanced Diet

A balanced diet is one of the basic principles of proper nutrition. It is a simple yet essential pillar in building good health. A balanced meal should contain all the required nutrients – carbohydrates, proteins, vitamins, and water –in correct proportions.

Taking a balanced diet requires discipline. Regardless of how much you love one type of food, you cannot eat it alone at the expense of other meals. Diversified meals with different nutritional values are important to the body.

2. Eating Fresh Food Only.

Fresh food is that which is not stale. It is important to take fresh food because they are not contaminated with bacteria that accumulate over time due to poor storage. Stale food introduces bacteria to our bodies that will make us fall sick.

Poorly preserved food poses a risk to our health. Hotels and restaurants adhere to guidelines of proper food handling to prevent food poisoning to their customers. Taking fresh food reduces the risk of falling sick.

3. Drinking Plenty Of Water.

The body majorly consists of water. It is an important part of a balanced diet. Water helps us hydrate and stay fit. So important is water that our bodies require it more than it does food.

It is recommended to take eight glasses of water in a day for us to stay hydrated because it is excreted in large quantities and we need to replenish it. Taking plenty of water also helps improve our skin tone.

4. Doing Physical Exercise.

Physical exercise is very important but often overlooked. Our bodies need exercise to stay fit and keep off lifestyle diseases. Exercises are also a form of therapy.

We sweat when we do intense workouts and excrete toxic substances from the body that would have otherwise been left inside the body. Sweating as a result of exercise is extremely healthy for our bodies.

5. Avoiding Stress.

Stress causes poor mental health. It is caused by the pressure to attain a certain threshold beyond our ability. We strain our minds and bodies when we push ourselves to the wall and we may eventually fall sick.

Poor mental health will catch up with our general health and if not taken care of early, it can irreversibly affect us.

6. Regular Health Check-Ups.

We should not go to the hospital only when we fall sick because it could be too late to save an already worse situation. We should visit a dentist bi-annually and an optician annually.

We should check our blood sugar levels and body pressure often to monitor any slight changes and address them before it is late. Good health is arrived at when we take care of all the variables affecting us.

7. Observing Health And Hygiene Standards.

There are health guidelines that are in place although hardly adhered to. They seem trivial but are very important in sustaining good health. We should not despise them.

Some guidelines are washing hands before meals and after visiting the toilet. We are also required to change our toothbrushes after every three months to promote dental hygiene.

8. Avoiding Self-Prescription Of Medicine.

It is common practice to buy medicine over the counter without a doctor's advice or prescription. It could have been prescribed to our friends or relatives and we think that we could also use it.

Doing this is wrong because there are many variables a medical officer considers before prescribing medicine that could not apply to us. Instead of getting well, we could worsen our health.

9. Do Not Share Medicine.

To ensure good health, do not share your medication with anyone without seeking professional advice. Not only could it not work for you, but you will also be endangering their health because you will tamper with their dosage.

Sharing of medicine could make you take expired medicine if the first person stopped taking it a long time ago and you use it without checking on the expiry date.

10. Understanding The Importance Of Good Health.

You only value what is important. When you understand the importance of good health, you will value it and observe that you do not lose it.

Health education is key to good health. Reading health literature and attending health talks will inspire you to work towards good health.

In conclusion, health is wealth. Take care of it early enough before it is unmanageable and costly.

Chapter 13:

How To Deal With Uncertainty?

How many of you are going through life right now but are dealing with a load of uncertainty that is weighing heavily on your mind?

You could be worrying about your career or work related matters: you wonder because the economy is taking a hit, whether you will still have your job tomorrow, whether your business would survive, or even if the economy is good, you are uncertain if you quit the current job you hate whether you are able to find another job in the near future or if you will even be competent in your new profession.

Or you could be worrying about your loved ones, your child who is studying overseas, or your spouse where they are working in the healthcare profession, working in the police or fire department, or even the military, where their lives are put at risk every single day, you worry if there will be one day that you might lose them and they won't come home.

Or you could be uncertain about smaller matters, matters such as if your date went well and if they would give you a call to ask you out again.

Whatever these may be, they all fall under the umbrella of uncertainty.

I would like to share with you uncertainties I faced personally and I would like to provide you with action steps to deal with them.

Recently I had been struggling with many uncertainties in my life. While they might not be your struggles I believe I would be able to provide more value if i shared my own story.

The first uncertainty I had was that I had recently restarted my publishing business after being away from it for a year, I was so afraid of what the market condition was like now, I was afraid of the competition, I was afraid I would fail again. I was afraid I would waste more of my time building up a business only to have it taken away from me.

The second worry I had was that I had also just begun taking my real estate exam to become a licensed realtor. I started having doubts about myself that I would ever become a competent realtor like my peers and I would look like a fool and I would feel disappointed with myself thereafter.

The next uncertainty I had was whether I would get the jobs that I applied for. I had decided to take on a part or full-time position to grow my professional career and I was afraid Whether the hours I spent on job applications would be in vain and that i would get no responses or even worse, rejections.

The final uncertainty was with stocks. Due to the incredible market volatility, I couldn't sleep properly every night because I wasn't sure what was gonna happen tmr. Whether I was gonna lose money while i was asleep.

I went about days with all these negative thoughts looming in my mind. It affected my sleep, my well-being, and my happiness. I started becoming dreary, unhappy, and lifeless. I spent 80% of my waking hours with these fears and doubts, and constantly beating myself up for feeling this way and it only made matters worse.

One day I decided it was enough. I took a deep breath and started collecting myself. I had had enough and I was so done with feeling these uncertainty and feeling sorry for myself.

I made the decision to accept my struggles, that they were a part of life and that there was no point in worrying about it. I decided it that I would just work hard on these areas, keep doing my best, and that whatever outcomes doesn't matter because I've given it my all. And finally I decided to live my day to the fullest and just be grateful that I even get to have the opportunity to pursue these ventures. After going through this process day in and day out, I became more at peace with myself. I started feeling less anxiety and adopted a more optimistic and positive mindset.

Here's what I realized. Uncertainty is born out of fear. This could be fear of losing someone, fear of the unknown, or even fear of failure. I had immense fears of failure that it crippled me to a really low point in my life. And the only way to overcome fear is first to accept that it is normal to be fearful, and then after to not let that fear get in the way of your happiness because life is too short for you to spend in a state of fearfulness. Rather, spend your time feeling grateful for your life and just try your best in everything that you do. Keep working on your dreams as if it were your last day on this earth, keep loving your spouse or child as though it was their last day on this earth, and ask yourself, is this how you would want to spend your time letting fear and uncertainty feed on your happiness? Or would you rather cherish every single moment you have with yourself and your family, and to live life with abundance instead.

This is my challenge to you. Uncertainty can only cripple you if you let it. Focus on your journey, your path, and trust in the process. But most importantly, Trust in yourself, believe in yourself even if no one else will. You owe that much love and compassion to yourself. I know you can do it.

Chapter 14:

9 Tips To Reduce Stress

Stress and anxiety are common experiences for most people. In fact, 70% of adults in the United States say they feel stress or anxiety daily. Here are 16 simple ways to relieve stress and anxiety.

1. Exercise

Exercise is one of the most important things you can do to combat stress. It might seem contradictory, but putting physical stress on your body through exercise can relieve mental stress. The benefits are strongest when you exercise regularly. People who exercise regularly are less likely to experience anxiety than those who don't exercise. Activities such as walking or jogging that involve repetitive movements of large muscle groups can be particularly stress relieving.

2. Consider supplements

Several supplements promote stress and anxiety reduction. Here is a brief overview of some of the most common ones:

Lemon balm: Lemon balm is a member of the mint family that has been studied for its anti-anxiety effects.

Omega-3 fatty acids: One study showed that medical students who received omega-3 supplements experienced a 20% reduction in anxiety symptoms.

Ashwagandha: Ashwagandha is an herb used in Ayurvedic medicine to treat stress and anxiety. Several studies suggest that it's effective.

Green tea: Green tea contains many polyphenol antioxidants which provide health benefits. It may lower stress and anxiety by increasing serotonin levels.

Valerian: Valerian root is a popular sleep aid due to its tranquilizing effect. It contains valerenic acid, which alters gamma-aminobutyric acid (GABA) receptors to lower anxiety.

Some supplements can interact with medications or have side effects, so you may want to consult with a doctor if you have a medical condition.

3. Light a candle

Using essential oils or burning a scented candle may help reduce your feelings of stress and anxiety.

Some scents are especially soothing. Here are some of the most calming scents:

- Lavender
- Rose
- Vetiver
- Bergamot
- Roman chamomile
- Neroli
- Frankincense
- Orange or orange blossom
- Geranium

Using scents to treat your mood is called aromatherapy. Several studies show that aromatherapy can decrease anxiety and improve sleep.

4. Reduce your caffeine intake

Caffeine is a stimulant found in coffee, tea, chocolate and energy drinks. High doses can increase anxiety. People have different thresholds for how much caffeine they can tolerate. If you notice that caffeine makes you jittery or anxious, consider cutting back. Although many studies show that coffee can be healthy in moderation, it's not for everyone. In general, five or fewer cups per day is considered a moderate amount.

5. Write it down

One way to handle stress is to write things down. While recording what you're stressed about is one approach, another is jotting down what you're grateful for. Gratitude may help relieve stress and anxiety by focusing your thoughts on what's positive in your life.

6. Chew gum

For a super easy and quick stress reliever, try chewing a stick of gum. One study showed that people who chewed gum had a greater sense of wellbeing and lower stress. One possible explanation is that chewing gum causes brain waves similar to those of relaxed people. Another is that chewing gum promotes blood flow to your brain. Additionally, one recent study found that stress relief was greatest when people chewed more strongly.

7. Spend time with friends and family

Social support from friends and family can help you get through stressful times. Being part of a friend network gives you a sense of belonging and self-worth, which can help you in tough times. One study found that for women in particular, spending time with friends and children helps release oxytocin, a natural stress reliever. This effect is called "tend and befriend," and is the opposite of the fight-or-flight response. Keep in mind that both men and women benefit from friendship. Another study found that men and women with the fewest social connections were more likely to suffer from depression and anxiety.

8. Laugh

It's hard to feel anxious when you're laughing. It's good for your health, and there are a few ways it may help relieve stress: Relieving your stress response. Relieving tension by relaxing your muscles.

In the long term, laughter can also help improve your immune system and mood. A study among people with cancer found that people in the laughter intervention group experienced more stress relief than those who were simply distracted. Try watching a funny TV show or hanging out with friends who make you laugh.

9. Learn to say no

Try not to take on more than you can handle. Saying no is one way to control your stressors.

Chapter 15:

How To Train Yourself to Be Optimistic and Positive

Positive thinking brings with it a whole host of benefits, such as better wellbeing and better sleep. To start reaping these benefits, check out how you can train your brain to be optimistic.

While many of us believe our happiness – or lack thereof – is based on external things, we're often the ones holding ourselves back. Many of us go through our days feeding ourselves negative messages we may not even be aware of, convincing ourselves we're "not good enough", "not clever enough" or "not attractive enough". To start thinking more positively, you need to change these messages. Try to look out for negative thoughts that pop into your head and replace them with positive messages. Write down some8 positive mantras and repeat them on a daily basis.

Most of us are happy to acknowledge other people's successes and accomplishments; however, when it comes to our own, we frequently play them down or ignore them entirely. To start thinking more positively about yourself, you need to regularly remind yourself of what you have – and can – achieve. Stop listening to your inner critic, reflect on your past achievements, and start to really appreciate your success and what you have to offer.

If you want to become an optimist, it can help to find yourself a positive role model. Whether it is a colleague, close friend or even a celebrity, think of the most unflappable, cheerful person you can. For the next few weeks, do an experiment and try to take a walk in their shoes. Whenever negativity starts creeping in or you find yourself in a difficult situation, think: "what would (insert name of chosen optimist) do?" Answer honestly, then try to follow suit.

It's important to remember that it isn't events themselves that make us unhappy, it is our interpretation and reaction to them, and while you can't always change events, you can change your response. When negative situations occur, try to reframe them by focusing on the positives or what you can learn from the situation. Maybe you have gained inner strength and resilience, grown closer to a friend through sharing your heartbreak or learned something about yourself. Try your best to focus on what you have learned and gained from your experience rather on than what you have lost.

When things don't go right in life, optimists tend to view each incident as an isolated event, while pessimists often look out for patterns of bad luck and think "if it happened once, it'll happen again". However, it is important not to try to predict the future based on what has happened before. Remember that a plan or relationship failing doesn't make you a failure and just because something disappointing has happened once (or more) it doesn't mean it will happen again.

What is gone is gone, and how you deal with the aftermath is the most important thing. There is no point apportioning blame, either on yourself or others. You have the power to change a situation and move on. It is so easy to say 'I should have done things differently' with the benefit of hindsight. However, if bad things have happened, look at tomorrow as exactly what it is — a new day — in which good things can happen, if you let them.

Chapter 16:

10 Habits of Amancio Ortega Gaona

Names like Warren Buffet and Bill Gates are household names, but do you know Amancio Ortega? Amancio is indeed one of the world's wealthiest fashion mogul. He founded Inditex, which is best known for Zara fashion and other men's and women's retail clothing, footwear, and home textiles businesses.

He is regarded as a pioneer in fast fashion thanks to his investment's eye. Zara's fashions are inspired by fashion show looks but are priced affordably to the average person. How did he get to where he is now? Here are 10 habits of Amancio Ortega.

1. Speed Is Entirely Everything

Ortega's "fast fashion" strategy demonstrates that speed is all you need to be ahead of your competitors and gain a market advantage. According to a business insider, a dress shown during Fashion Week can be found in Zara a few weeks later, while the same takes months to be displayed at a department store. His market aggressiveness is scheduled to design new clothes faster than anyone else in the market.

2. Good Things Comes With Patience

Although ten years may seem interminable when starting a business, it pays off. Being patient allows you to wait, observe, and decide when it is appropriate to act. It was after Zara went international 10 years later after trying different business approaches that Ortega broke through. Accordingly, all you need to do is take a step back, regroup, and look for better solutions.

3. It is About What Customers Want

Ortega's fashion sense stems from his observation of what people wear and listening to what they want. As his guiding business model, he does not base his inventory on runway shows but rather on what customers want. The customer must remain your primary focus, both in developing your new designs and the related activities.

4. Introverts Are Also Entrepreneurs

Many successful entrepreneurs, such as Ortega, are not extroverts, as might be expected in their line of work. Ortega once stated that even if you aren't the party's life, you can still run a successful business. He is the type of person who avoids speaking to the press at all costs, so little is known about him.

5. Be Modest and Humble

Ortega's journey is a classic rags to-riches story, but he has remained true to his humble beginnings. He dropped out of school to start making money. According to The Telegraph, he has never had an office because he prefers working very close with his employees. A humble beginning does not preclude you from becoming successful, and success does not preclude you from remaining modest and humble. Those qualities can be extremely beneficial in both your personal and professional life.

6. Keep On Innovating

As Ortega puts it, "the worst thing you can do is becoming self-satisfied." Success is never guaranteed, so don't be satisfied with what you've already done. If you want to innovate, don't be concerned more with the outcome than the process.

7. Maintain Control Over Supply Chain

When you focus on a specific supply chain, you will undoubtedly respond to new trends accordingly. While many fashion companies stock clothing made in China due to low labor costs, Inditex sources most of its products from Spain, Portugal, and Morocco, according to The Economist in 2012. Ortega's stores only sell what customers want, so there are no unsold items.

8. Keep in Mind What Motivates You

Remembering what makes you wake up early in the morning to do what you do is your drive for success. Take, for instance, Ortega's childhood; he witnessed his mother being denied credit at a grocery store when he was young. At this moment, he was motivated to start working right away so that his family wouldn't have to be in such a situation again.

9. Age Is Not a Limit to Success

Sometimes you're led to believe that you must be successful at a young age, much like Steve Jobs or Mark Zuckerberg. However, Ortega founded Zara when he was nearly 40 years old. While that isn't particularly old by most people's standards, it isn't your typical twenty- or thirty-something millionaire story. It's reassuring to know that it's never too late to pursue your dreams and ambitions, as Ortega did.

10. Enjoy the Finer Things in Life

Despite his modesty and humbleness, Ortega also engages in some fun activities. He spends his free time horse riding and owns a horse riding center in Finisterre, Spain. He also owns a high-end Audi A8 sedan. It's okay to have time for yourself; spend money vacationing if you can afford it.

Conclusion

Amancio Ortega Gaona's success story is truly inspiring, as he rose from nothing to become one of Europe's richest businessmen and fashion pioneers. No matter small you start, you'll surely reach there. But only if you're motivated enough to see it.

Chapter 17:

How To Deal With Feelings of Unworthiness

Today we're going to talk about a topic that I hope none of you struggle with. But if you do, I hope to bring some light into your life today. Because i too have had to deal with such feelings before, as recently as a year ago actually.

So before we get into the solutions, we must first understand where these feelings of unworthiness comes form. And we must be aware of them before we can make changes in our lives that brings us out of that state of mind.

Let's start with my life, maybe you will understand the kinds of struggles that I had gone through that led me to feeling unworthy.

Just about 3 years ago, I started my entrepreneurial journey, a journey that was full of excitement and curiousity. After being through a couple of internships at a company, i knew the corporate life wasn't really my thing, and i set out on my own path to making money online... To see if i could find a way to have an income without having to work a 9-5 job. The start was rough as I had no experience whatsoever. But over time i started to find a bit of footing and I made some decent income here and there that would sustain my livelihood for a while. As I was starting to see some success, my "world" came crashing down as something happened with the small business that I had spent almost 3 years building up. And suddenly my income was gone. And I realized I had nothing to show for my 3 years of work. It left me feeling incredibly depressed... Although it doesnt sound like the end of the world to many of you, i felt like i had been set back many years behind my peers who were by then already steadily climbing up the corporate ladder. Feelings that I had made a grave mistake in terms of career choice started creeping up on me. As I tried to figure out what to do with my life, I couldn't help but compare my income to the income that my friends were making. And I felt did feel worthless, and inferior. And I started questioning my whole journey and life choices up till that point.

I started wondering if I was ever going to climb my way back up again, if I would ever figure out how these things actually worked, and all those negative thoughts came day in and out. Eating me alive inside.

It was only after I had done some introspection did I finally started to learn to love myself. And to learn that my journey is unique and mine alone. That I didn't need to, and must not, compare myself to others, did i really start to feel worthy again. I started to believe in my own path, and I felt proud that I had dared to try something that most of my peers were afraid to even try. I found new qualities in myself that I didn't knew I had and I started to forge a new path for myself in my own entrepreneurial journey. Eventually my experience making money online helped me claw my way back up the income ladder, and I have never looked backed since.

For me personally, the one thing that I could take away from my own experience with unworthiness, is to not compare yourself with others. You will never be happy comparing with your peers on income, relationship status, number of friends, number of followers on social media, and all that random things. If you always look at your friends in that way, you will always feel inferior because there will always be someone better than you. Sure you can look to them for inspiration and tips, but never feel that they are superior to you in anyway.. because you are unique in your own beautiful way. You should focus on your own journey and how you can be a better version of yourself. Your peers might have different sets of skills, talents, and expertise, that helped them excel in their fields, but you have your own talents too that you should exploit. You never know what you can achieve until you truly believe in yourself and fully utilise your potential.

For you, your struggle with unworthiness could stem from the way your parents compare you to your siblings, or feeling hopeless trying to find love in this cruel world, or being rejected by companies in your Job applications, or rejection by a potential suitor. These are all valid things that can bring us down. But never let these people tell you what you can or cannot do. Prove to them that you are worthy by constantly improving yourself, mentally, physically, health wise, being emotionally resilient, grow your wisdom, and always love yourself. People cannot love you if you do not love yourself first. That is a quote that i believe very deeply.

No amount of validation from external sources can match the love that I decide to give to myself first.

If you find yourself in situations where you are being bombarded with negativity, whether it be from friends or family, i suggest you take a step back from these people. Find a community where your achievements are celebrated and appreciated, and where you can also offer the same amount of encouragement to others. Join meetup groups in your area with people of similar interests and just enjoy the journey. You will get there eventually if you believe in yourself.

So I challenge each and every one of you to always choose yourself first, look at your own journey as a unique path, different from everybody else, follow your dreams, take action, and never give up. That is the only way to prove to yourself and to the world that you are the most worthy person on the planet.

Chapter 18:

How To Find Motivation

Today we're going to talk about a topic that hopefully will help you find the strength and energy to do the work that you've told yourself you've wanted or needed to but always struggle to find the one thing that enables you to get started and keep going. We are going to help you find motivation.

In this video, I am going to break down the type of tasks that require motivation into 2 distinct categories. Health and fitness, and work. As I believe that these are the areas where most of you struggle to stay motivated. With regards to family, relationships, and other areas, i dont think motivation is a real problem there.

For all of you who are struggling to motivate yourself to do things you've been putting off, for example getting fit, going to the gym, motivation to stay on a diet, to keep working hard on that project, to study for your exams, to do the chores, or to keep working on your dreams... All these difficult things require a huge amount of energy from us day in and day out to be consistent and to do the work.

I know... it can be incredibly difficult. Having experienced these ups and downs in my own struggle with motivation, it always starts off swimmingly... When we set a new year's resolution, it is always easy to think that we will stick to our goal in the beginning. We are super motivated to go do the gym to lose those pounds, and we go every single day for about a week... only to give up shortly after because we either don't see results, or we just find it too difficult to keep up with the regime.

Same goes for starting a new diet... We commit to doing these things for about a week, but realize that we just simply don't like the process and we give up as well...

Finding motivation to study for an important exam or working hard on work projects are a different kind of animal. As these are things that have a deadline. A sense of urgency that if we do not achieve our desired result, we might fail or get fired from our company. With these types of tasks, most of us are driven by fear, and fear becomes our motivator... which is also not healthy for us as stress hormones builds within us as we operate that way, and we our health pays for it.

Let's start with tackling the first set of tasks that requires motivation. And i would classify this at the health and fitness level. Dieting, exercise, going to the gym, eating healthily, paying attention to your sleep... All these things are very important, but not necessarily urgent to many of us. The deadline we set for ourselves to achieve these health goals are arbitrary. Based on the images we see of models, or people who seem pretty fit around us, we set an unrealistic deadline for ourselves to achieve those body goals. But more often than not, body changes don't happen in days or weeks for most of us by the way we train. It could take up to months or years... For those celebrities and fitness models you see on Instagram or movies, they train almost all day by personal trainers. And their deadline is to look good by the start of shooting for the movie. For most of us who have day jobs, or don't train as hard, it is unrealistic to expect we can achieve that body in the same amount of time. If we only set aside 1 hour a day to exercise, while we may get gradually fitter, we shouldn't expect that amazing transformation to happen so quickly. It is why so many of us set ourselves up for failure.

To truly be motivated to keep to your health and fitness goals, we need to first define the reasons WHY we even want to achieve these results in the first place. Is it to prove to yourself that you have discipline? Is it to look good for your wedding photoshoot? Is it for long term health and fitness? Is it so that you don't end up like your relatives who passed too soon because of their poor health choices? Is it to make yourself more attractive so that you can find a man or woman in your life? Or is it just so that you can live a long and healthy life, free of medical complications that plague most seniors by the time they hit their 60s and 70s? What are YOUR reasons WHY you want to keep fit? Only after you know these reasons, will you be able to truly set a realistic deadline for your health goals. For those that are in it for a better health overall until their ripe old age, you will realize that this health goal is a life long thing. That you need to treat it as a journey that will take years and decades. And small changes each day will add up. Your motivator is not to go to the gym 10 hours a day for a week, but to eat healthily consistently and exercise regularly every single day so that you will still look and feel good 10, 20, 30, 50 years, down the road.

And for those that need an additional boost to motivate you to keep the course, I want you to find an accountability partner. A friend that will keep you in check. And hopefully a friend that also has the same health and fitness goals as you do. Having this person will help remind you not to let yourself and this person down. Their presence will hopefully motivate you to not let your guard down, and their honesty in pointing out that you've been slacking will keep you in check constantly that you will do as you say.

And if you still require an additional boost on top of that, I suggest you print and paste a photo of the body that you want to achieve and the idol that you wish to emulate in terms of having a good health and fitness on a board where you can see every single day. And write down your reasons why beside it. That way, you will be motivated everytime you walk past this board to keep to your goals always.

Now lets move on to study and work related tasks. For those with a fixed 9-5 job and deadlines for projects and school related work, your primary motivator right now is fear. Which as we established earlier, is not exactly healthy. What we want to do now is to change these into more positive motivators. Instead of thinking of the consequences of not doing the task, think of the rewards you would get if you completed it early. Think of the relief you will feel knowing that you had not put off the work until the last minute. And think of the benefits that you will gain... less stress, more time for play, more time with your family, less worry that you have to cram all the work at the last possible minute, and think of the good results you will get, the opportunities that you will have seized, not feeling guilty about procrastinations... and any other good stuff that you can think of. You could also reward yourself with a treat or two for completing the task early. For example buying your favourite food, dessert, or even gadgets. All these will be positive motivators that will help you get the ball moving quicker so that you can get to those rewards sooner. Because who likes to wait to have fun anyway?

Now I will move on to talk to those who maybe do not have a deadline set by a boss or teacher, but have decided to embark on a new journey by themselves. Whether it be starting a new business, getting your accounting done, starting a new part time venture.. For many of these tasks, the only motivator is yourself. There is no one breathing down your neck to get the job done fast and that could be a problem in itself. What should we do in that situation? I believe with this, it is similar to how we motivate ourselves in the heath and fitness goals. You see, sheer force doesn't always work sometimes. We need to establish the reasons why we want to get all these things done early in life. Would it be to fulfil a dream that we always had since we were a kid? Would it be to earn an extra side income to travel the world? Would it be to prove to yourself that you can have multiple streams of income? Would it to become an accomplished professional in a new field? Only you can define your reasons WHY you want to even begin and stay on this new path in the first place. So only you can determine why and how you can stay on the course to eventually achieve it in the end.

Similarly for those of you who need additional help, I would highly recommend you to get an accountability partner. Find someone who is in similar shoes as you are, whether you are an entrepreneur, or self-employed, or freelance, find someone who can keep you in check, who knows exactly what you are going through, and you can be each other's pillars of support when one of you finds yourself down and out. Or needs a little pick me up. There is a strong motivator there for you to keep you on course during the rough time.

And similar to health and fitness goal, find an image on the web that resonates with the goal you are trying to achieve. Whether it might be to buy a new house, or to become successful, i want that image to always be available to you to look at every single day. That you never forget WHY you began the journey. This constant reminder should light a fire in you each and everyday to get you out of your mental block and to motivate you to take action consistently every single day.

So I challenge each and every one of you to find motivation in your own unique way. Every one of you have a different story to tell, are on different paths, and no two motivators for a person are the same. Go find that one thing that would ignite a fire on your bottom everytime you look at it. Never forget the dream and keep staying the course until you reach the summit.

Chapter 19:

The Struggle With Time

Today we're going to talk about a topic that isn't commonly looked at in depth. But it is one that we might hopefully find a new appreciation for. And that is TIME.

Time is a funny thing, we are never really aware of it and how much of a limited resource it really is until we get a rude awakening. Most commonly when our mortality is tested. Whether it be a health scare, an accident, a death of a loved one, a death of a pet, we always think we have more time before that. That we will always have time to say i love you, to put off the things we always told ourselves we needed to do, to start making that change, to spend time with the people that mean the most to us.

As we go about our days, weeks and months, being bothered and distracted by petty work, by our bosses, colleagues, trying to climb the corporate ladder, we forget to stop and check in on our fiends and family... We forget that their time may be running out, and that we may not have as much time with them as we think we do, until it is too late, and then we regret not prioritising them first. All the money that we made could not ever buy back the time we have lost with them. And that is something we have to live with if we ever let that happen.

The other funny thing about time is that if we don't set it aside for specific tasks, if we don't schedule anything, we will end up wasting it on something mindless. Whether it be browsing social media endlessly, or bingeing on television, we will never run out of things to fill that time with. Can you imagine that even though time is so precious, we willingly sacrifice and trade it in for self isolation in front of our TVs and computers for hours on end. Sometimes even for days? Or even on mobile games. Some being so addictive that it consumes most of our waking hours if we are not careful.

Our devices have become dangerous time wasters. It is a tool Shea its literally sapping the living energy out of us. Which is why some responsible companies have started implementing new features that help us keep track of our screen time. To keep us in check, and to not let our children get sucked into this black hole that we might struggle to climb out of.

I believe the biggest struggle with time that we all have is how to spend it in such a way that we can be happy without feeling guilty. Guilty of not spending it wisely. And I believe the best way to start is to start defining the things that you need to do, and the things that you want to do. And then striking a balance. To set equal amounts of time into each activity so that it doesn't overwhelm or underwhelm you. Spend onc hour on each activity each day that you feel will have an impact on your life in a meaningful way, and you can spend your time on television or games without remorse.

So I challenge each of you to make the most of your time. SPending time with loved ones always come first, followed by your goals and dreams, and then leisure activities. Never the other way around. That way you can be at the end of your life knowing that you had not wasted the most precious commodity that we are only given a finite amount of. Money can't buy back your youth, your health, or time with loved ones, so don't waste it.

Chapter 20:

How To Succeed In Life Before Quitting.

Getting rid of a job is always risky, especially if you want to succeed in life. Sometimes we have to choose our satisfactory activity even if we are settled for something else. But you have to keep in mind that these risks might be worth pursuing your dreams. You should have confidence in yourself if you are letting go of your stable job. You are starting by taking small baby steps and keeping a clear idea in your mind of what you want or if quitting your job is the right decision.

When wanting to quit a full-time job, you need to make sure of some things first. One of them is financial stability. It's not something you can leave on its own. Taking care of your finances should be your first step as it will help you in further needs. Try not to ask for help much. Make yourself capable of purchasing your needs and wants.

To be a successful person, the most important thing is not to be afraid of failure. You have to plant courage and confidence in your mind. Quitting will be easier when you know what you are doing. It keeps you aware of your needs and makes your decision stronger. You cannot second guess yourself if you make the right choice. Be willing to fail ever once in a while.

Positivity in life is an easier way to be successful. Take everything lightly and make sure that negativity gets ignored. You cannot get discouraged if people don't support your ideas and goals. Suppose you feel like you should quit. Go for it. The world will not see the journey, but the results will be visualized clearly for them. So, keep positivity in your mind and heart.

Becoming a successful person comes with a lot to take in, and it might not be as easy as it will have seemed. So, the smartest move that anyone can make is to take their time while making any decision in this regard. So should weigh all of your options while keeping your mental and physical health in check. Choose the best one for yourself always.

You should be ready for anything that comes your way. Don't be scared of rejection. Don't be scared of others' opinions. Even ask for advice from someone if you need help in deciding. Ask your superiors for guidance in this regard. Let people motivate you for a greater cause. And better, motivate yourself. The secret to success is to enjoy your work. If you work thinking that you will earn only or become powerful only, you are wrong. You will be stuck in one place for a long time. You need to make sure to have fun along the way. That way, everything you do will be worth it.

Becoming successful before quitting can be quite challenging, but that is one way to become yourself. You are getting a focused view of what you want in life and how you'll work things out. Just make sure to have all the right ingredients you'll need to quit one part of your life to start a new one. And hopefully a better part of your life for yourself.

Chapter 21:

Get Your Brain To Focus On What Matters

The very first step r the very first feeling close to success is that you are capable of visualizing it every day and every night. If your brain is so focused on what matters and has a much clearer vision of the final product of your efforts, then you have the best friend you could ever wish to see.

If your brain can do this, you have done the biggest and most difficult task of your life, that is, training your brain to think of things just as your will dictates you.

We live in an era of technology so reliable yet also disturbingly manipulative that we cannot think of a single thing more important than our phone if we lose one.

Think about it, You wake up on the alarm of your phone. You snooze it and you check your feed. You check IGN, Twitter, and other social media platforms to check if someone approached you or if something more havoc has occurred anywhere on the planet. We are always so dependant on the technology around us that we cannot take an hour out of this ecosystem to make something more meaningful with our time.

We are often told that we have a limited time on this planet and there are a lot more things to achieve in life. But what do we do to make things seem more meaningful than what we do on our phones?

So what to do in such an era of technology to be more productive?

I would say, stop keeping your phone in your pocket. I can assure you this idea is not as stupid as it may sound initially. But hear me for a second.

We have a different screen for a different environment. We use an IPad or a Tablet when we want to relax on a couch for Netflix. We use our laptops for office work strictly. We use a desktop for gaming and stuff. But our phones, we carry everywhere.

We wake up with it and we sleep with it. We cannot commute without it, which I know is justified but we don't commute all day long. So why do you need to keep it in your pocket for the rest of the day?

Start this practice today for a better chance. Use a traditional alarm clock over your phone. When you want to read the news over breakfast, use a newspaper. When you are in the office, put your phone on your desk and switch it to the meeting.

Life has a lot of important things for you to do. You need to take some time out of everything you do for yourself in a day and devote some of it to your friends family and your other half.

How much more time do you need for yourself, when you sleep a third of your day just so you can function properly the next day. So start thinking of new ways to use your time for making more money rather than sulking over others' success just by looking at some social media post.

Chapter 22:

10 Habits of Sergey Brin

When you say "the apple doesn't fall far from the tree," you're undoubtedly referring to Serge Brin's facts. Although he paused his Ph.D. studies to start Google, the man appears to have followed in his parents' footsteps. Sergey comes from a well-educated family; his mother is a NASA researcher, and his father is a math professor.

Sergey Brin is the co-founder of Google and Alphabet Inc., a computer scientist, and a highly successful entrepreneur. The Russian techie met Larry Page while pursuing his Ph.D. studies, and they both dropped out to start Google. Despite being a latecomer to the search game, Google now reigns supreme.

Here are 10 Habits of Sergey Brine.

1. Disable Temptation

Just like Sergey Brin, when handling a matter of great importance, practices self-control and disable any temptations or distractions. Disable your phone when necessary, install apps that help you maintain control to stay focused. Having a habit Stacker is also an excellent tool for helping you build the focus needed.

2. Don't Think About Money.

When it comes to success, most people think of money. But when Brin and Larry were creating Google, money was far from their minds. They wanted to create a search engine that people could rely on to get information on anything on the internet. Once you create something of value, be sure to rip greatness in the end as Brin is now.

3. Worry Less About the Roadblocks

Brin once said that the success journey is a journey multiple failures. Many young people are prone to seeing massive mountains, but he sees only a small one to climb. It's all about your perfective to approaching life and focusing on overcoming minor problems. The more you focus on the mountains, the more anxious you become and the less productive you'll be.

4. Shut the Door

Increasing the ability to stay "locked into something" is extremely important to Sergey, which drives Google's development. Close the door, both literally and metaphorically. This entails preventing the outside world from interfering with your project's progress. When you close your door, you are signaling to the world that you are working.

5. Greatness Comes From Unexpected Places

Has anyone ever made fun of you for unexpected reasons? Has anyone ever questioned your abilities because of who they perceived you to be? Say no more – you already know the truth and your capabilities. Sergey and his co-founder made Google from their dorm room, and it took off quickly such that by 2000, it had collected over one billion URLs. You can achieve great things no matter where you come from, where you started, or now.

6. Think Big

Google is one of the world's most excellent, fast, and diverse companies, thanks to Sergey Brin, a daring thinker, and entrepreneur. Google is so flexible and abstract that you wouldn't know its following ideas and inventions. The idea, as Brin insists, is to think big or go home! Without an optimistic attitude or charismatic intuition, your thoughts are not worth a dime.

7. Work With the Appropriate Team

You need a great team working for you, just as Sergey Brin focuses on getting the best talents working for Google for better results. It doesn't matter if you have a small or large company; you can benefit from size. When you go from 1–10 people, you have no idea who they are. At that point, the best course of action would be to continue growing and reaping the benefits of scale.

8. Be an Ambitious Creator

According to the New York Times, Brin may have played a significant role in developing several projects as Google evolved from just a search engine to a large company. He was the key driver behind the most ambitious projects, including Google+, self-driving cars, smart contact lenses, and smart glasses. All you need is an intense desire and determination to put your ideas into action.

9. Be Inquisitive

A curious person like Sergey Brin will always find a thousand reasons to achieve the goals. As he says, "when a dream appears, seize it," it is best to go extra crazy to achieve what you believe in. Just ensure you don't give up on your dreams and strive for the best.

10. Apply Brilliance

Anyone who knows Sergey knows that he truly believes in using his power and knowledge for the greater good. The Economist dubbed him the "Enlightenment Man" for his commitment to using science and logic to solve major global issues. Everyone wants to be successful, but when you see yourself as an innovator, ethical, and trustworthy person, you will be remembered as a game-changer, just as Brin wants to be remembered.

Conclusion

It's pretty clear that Sergey Brin is an intellect personality. His abilities and talents are so unique that it's understandable to envy him or want to be like him. However, once you focus on changing the world, the more likely you'll be recognized among the greatest.

Chapter 23:

How To Worry Less

How many of you worry about little things that affect the way you go about your day? That when you're out with your friends having a good time or just carrying out your daily activities, when out of nowhere a sudden burst of sadness enters your heart and mind and immediately you start to think about the worries and troubles you are facing. It is like you're fighting to stay positive and just enjoy your day but your mind just won't let you. It becomes a tug of war or a battle to see who wins?

How many of you also lose sleep because your mind starts racing at bedtime and you're flooded with sad feelings of uncertainty, despair, worthlessness or other negative emotions that when you wake up, that feeling of dread immediately overwhelms you and you just feel like life is too difficult and you just dont want to get out of bed.

Well If you have felt those things or are feeling those things right now, I want to tell you you're not alone. Because I too struggle with those feelings or emotions on a regular basis.

At the time of writing this, I was faced with many uncertainties in life. My business had just ran into some problems, my stocks weren't doing well, I had lost money, my bank account was telling me I wasn't good enough, but most importantly, i had lost confidence. I had lost the ability to face each day with confidence that things will get better. I felt that i was worthless and that bad things will always happen to me. I kept seeing the negative side of things and it took a great deal of emotional toll on me. It wasn't like i chose to think and feel these things, but they just came into my mind whenever they liked. It was like a parasite feeding off my negative energy and thriving on it, and weakening me at the same time.

Now your struggles may be different. You may have a totally different set of circumstances and struggles that you're facing, but the underlying issue is the same. We all go through times of despair, worry, frustration, and uncertainty. And it's totally normal and we shouldn't feel ashamed of it but to accept that it is a part of life and part of our reality.

But there are things we can do to minimise these worries and to shift to a healthier thought pattern that increases our ability to fight off these negative emotions.

I want to give you 5 actionable steps that you can take to worry less and be happier. And these steps are interlinked that can be carried out in fluid succession for the greatest benefit to you. But of course you can choose whichever ones speaks the most to you and it is more important that you are able to practice any one of these steps consistently rather than doing all 5 of them haphazardly. But I want to make sure I give you all the tools so that you can make the best decisions for yourself.

Try this with me right now as I go through these 5 steps and experience the benefit for yourself instead of waiting until something bad happens.

The very first step is simple. Just breathe. When a terrible feeling of sadness rushes into your body out of nowhere, take that as a cue to close your eyes, stop whatever you are doing, and take 5 deep breathes through your nose. Breathing into your chest and diaphragm. Deep breathing has the physiological benefit of calming your nerves and releasing tension in the body and it is a quick way to block out your negative thoughts. Pause the video if you need to do practice your deep breathing before we move on.

And as you deep breathe, begin the second step. Which is to practice gratefulness. Be grateful for what you already have instead of what you think u need to have to be happy. You could be grateful for your dog, your family, your friends, and whatever means the most to you. And if you cannot think of anything to be grateful for, just be grateful that you are even alive and walking on this earth today because that is special and amazing in its own right.

Next is to practice love and kindness to yourself. You are too special and too important to be so cruel to yourself. You deserve to be loved and you owe it to yourself to be kind and forgiving. Life is tough as it is, don't make it harder. If you don't believe in yourself, I believe in you and I believe in your worthiness as a person that you have a lot left to give.

The fourth step is to Live Everyday as if it were your last. Ask yourself, will you still want to spend your time worrying about things out of your control if it was your last day on earth? Will you be able to forgive yourself if you spent 23 out of the last 24 hours of your life worrying? Or will you choose to make the most out of the day by doing things that are meaningful and to practice love to your family, friends, and yourself?

Finally, I just want you to believe in yourself and Have hope that whatever actions you are taking now will bear fruition in the future. That they will not be in vain. That at the end of the day, you have done everything to the very best of your ability and you will have no regrets and you have left no stone unturned.

How do you feel now? Do you feel that it has helped at least a little or even a lot in shaping how you view things now? That you can shift your perspective and focus on the positives instead of the worries?

If it has worked for you today, I want to challenge you to consistently practice as many of these 5 steps throughout your daily lives every single day. When you feel a deep sadness coming over you, come back to this video if you need guidance, or practice these steps if you remember them on your own.

Chapter 24:

Get Rid of Worry and Focus On The Work

Worry is the active process of bringing one's fears into reality.

Worrying about problems halts productivity by taking your mind off the work in hand.

If you're not careful, a chronic state of worrying can lead you down a dark path that you might find hard to get out of.

Always focus on the required work and required action towards your dream.

Anything could happen, good or bad,

but if you remain focused and do the work despite the problems,

you will through with persistence and succeed.

Always keep your mind on the goal,

your eyes on the prize.

Have an unwavering faith in your abilities no matter what.

Plan for the obvious obstacles that could stand in your way,

but never worry about them until you have to face them.

Tackle it with confidence as they come and move forward with pride.

Problems are bound to arise.

Respond to them necessarily along the way, if they actually happen.

After all, most worries never make it into reality.

Instead focus on what could go right.

Focus on how you can create an environment that will improve your chances of success.

You have the power over your own life and direction.

As children we dreamed big.

We didn't think about all the things that could go wrong.

As children we only saw the possibilities.

We were persistent in getting what we wanted no matter the cost.

As adults we need to be reminded of that child-like faith.

To crush worry as if it were never there.

To only focus on the possibilities.

You cannot be positive and negative at the same time.

You cannot be worrying and hopeful of the future.

You cannot visualise your perfect life while worrying about everything that could go wrong.

Choose one.

Stick to it.

Choose to concentrate on the work.

The result will take care of your worries.

Catch yourself when you feel yourself beginning to worry about things.

Instead of dwelling on the problem, choose to double down on the action.

Stay focused and steadfast in the vision of your ultimate goal.

The work now that you must do is the stepping stones to your success.

The work now must have your immediate attention.

The work now requires you to cast worry aside in favour of concentration and focus.

How many stepping stones are you away?

What is next?

Push yourself every single day.

Because only you have the power to create your future.

If not, things will remain the same as they have always been.

Always have a clearly defined goal,

A strong measure of faith,

And an equally strong measure of persistence and grit.

These are the ingredients to creating the life you want.

A life of lasting happiness and success.

Take control instead of accepting things as they are.

Reject anything else that is not the goal that you've set for yourself.

Whatever goal you set, ten times it, and focus on it every day.

The focus will keep your mind on the work until you succeed.

There will be no time to worry when you are too busy taking constant action.

Always have the belief In your heart and soul that you will succeed.

Never let a grain of doubt cast a shadow in your eventual path to victory.

Focus is key to all.

What you focus on, you will create.

Worrying is worse than useless,

it is DETRIMENTAL to your future.

Take control of your thoughts.

When worry pops it's ugly head, force it out with a positive thought of your future.

Don't let the negative illusions of worry live rent-free in your mind.

You are in control here.

Of what you watch,

What you read,

What you listen too

And what you think.

What you think of consistently will become.

Focus on what you want, and how to get there is crucial for lasting happiness and success.

Chapter 25:

Don't Stay At Home

Today we're going to talk about why you should consider getting out of your house as much as possible, especially if you need to get work done, or if you have some other important personal projects that requires your undivided attention to complete.

For those that work full-time jobs, we all aspire to one day be able to work from home. We all dream of one day being able to just get up from our beds and walk over to our desks to begin work.

Having tried this myself for the last 4 years, I can safely tell you that staying at home isn't all that amazing as it has been talked up or hyped up to be.

While it may sound nice to be able to work from home, in reality, distractions are tough to avoid, and procrastination is one major killer of productivity at home. Many of us have made our homes the Center of entertainment and relaxation. We buy nice couches, TVs, beds, speakers, etc, and all these items around the house are temptations for us to slack off.

For those who are living with family, or who have pets, their presence could also disrupt our productivity.

Without people around us to motivate us to keep working hard, we tend to just tell ourselves "it's okay I'll just watch this one show and then I'll get back to work", and before we know it, it is 5pm and we haven't done a single thing.

Some people love it, some people hate it, but personally, I much prefer getting my butt out of the house and into a co-working space, a cafe, or a library, where I can visually see other people working hard, which motivates me to stay away from slacking off.

Having been doing regular journaling to measure my productivity, staying at home has always resulted in my worst daily performance no matter how hard I try to make my home environment the most conducive for work. Feeling like taking nap because my bed is right there, or watching a Netflix show on my big screen tv, has always been hard to resist. You will be surprised how many hours you are potentially losing from just indulging in any of these things.

For those who really has no choice but to work from home, either to save money, or because you need to take care of a family member. I would highly suggest that you optimise your environment to give yourself the greatest chance of success.

Dedicate a room that will be made into your study/work room, ensure that there is adequate and bright lighting, and to Keep all possible distractions outside the room. Putting your work desk in your bedroom is the worst thing you can do because you will blur the lines between rest and work if you mix the two things up in one tiny space. Not only will you feel sluggish working from your bedroom, but you might also develop sleep issues as well.

Not staying at home is still your best bet for success. Find a space outside where you can be focused and have the discipline to get yourself there every single day, no matter how tired or lethargic you feel. Once you leave the house, you have already won half the battle in getting your productivity under control.

Chapter 26:

Why You're Demotivated By Lack of Clarity

Clarity is key to achieving any lasting happiness or success.
Demotivation is almost certain without clarity.

Always have a clear vision of what you want and why you want it.
Every detail should be crystal clear as if it were real.
Because it is.
Mustn't reality first be built on a solid foundation of imagination.
Your skills in visualisation and imagination must be strong to build that foundation.

You must build it in the mind and focus on it daily.
You must believe in it with all your heart and your head will follow.
Create it in the mind and let your body build it in reality.
That is the process of creation.

You cannot create anything in reality without clarity in the mind.
Even to make a cup of coffee, you must first imagine making a cup of coffee.
It doesn't take as much clarity as creating an international company,
but focus and clarity are required nonetheless.

The big goals often take years of consistent focus, clarity and commitment.

That is why so few succeed.

Demotivation is a symptom of lack of direction.

To have direction you must have clarity.

To have clarity you must have a clearly defined vision of you future.

Once you have this vision, never accept anything less.

Clarity and vision will begin your journey,

but your arrival depends on stubbornness and persistence.

Before you start you must decide to never quit, no matter what happens.

Clarity of your why will decide this for you.

Is the pain you are about to endure stronger than your reasons?

If you are currently demoralised by lack of clarity,

sit down and decide what will really make you happy.

Once you have decided, begin to make it feel real with pictures around your house.

Listen to motivational music and speeches daily to build your belief in you.

Visit where you dream you will be one day.

Get a feel for your desired new life.

Create actions that will build clarity in your vision.

Let it help you adjust to your new and future reality.

Slowly adjust your vision upwards.
Never adjust downwards.
Never settle for less.

The more real your vision feels the more likely it will be.
Begin to visualise living it.
Before long you will be living it.

Adopt the mannerisms of someone who would be in that position.
When you begin to believe you are important, others will follow.
Carry yourself like a champion.
Soon you will be one.

Have clarity you have about who you are.
Have clarity about what you are going to do.
Motivate yourself to success.

Once you step on that path you will not want to return to the you of yesterday.
You will be committed to becoming even better tomorrow.
You will be committed to being the new person you've always known you could be.

Always strive to get another step closer to your vision.
Work until that vision becomes clearer each day.

Have faith that each week more opportunities for progression will present themselves to you.

Clarity is the key to your success.

Chapter 27:

Living Life Without Regrets.

As Mick Jagger once said, "the past is a great place and I don't want to erase it or to regret it, but I don't want to be its prisoner either." Regret is like an uninvited ghost, and it likes to make an appearance when we are at our lowest. It dwells in the back of our heads from time to time and reminds us of the things that we wish we had done differently in our lives. But, just like a million other things and emotions, regrets only stay with us if we feed on it and let it in. It can be A heavy burden for us to carry, so in order to get rid of this lingering ghost, it's essential that we first understand what we are actually regretting and why.

If your life were about to end tomorrow - if that drunk doesn't stop at the red light, or the meteor is headed right for your house, would you go into your memory and start seeing your regrets? Or would you just accept it all and wish that you had lived your life more freely? Trust me when I say this, it's really okay to screw up. We're not people who can't make any mistakes and be flawless. Take A hurdler in the olympics as an example; he knocks over about half of the hurdles in that 110 metres, and they don't even break stride. Because at the end, it's not about not knocking over any hurdles or running the perfect race, it all comes down to getting across the line. So don't ever fear or regret failing - you give it A shot, and that's all that matters in the end.

We all know how Michael Jordan struggled with his career. In his own words, "I've missed more than 9000 shots in my career. I've lost almost 3000 games. 26 times, I've been trusted to take the game winning shot and missed. I've failed over and over and over again in my life. And that's why I succeed." Had he given up in his first try, the world would have never known A legend like him. He must've had A thousand second thoughts every time he failed, he must've regretted opting basketball every time he lost A game, but he kept going and never gave up. We should have A similar outlook on our lives. No matter what we did in our past, or whatever our decisions were that led to what we are now, it all must have A connection or A meaning. We just have to stop, think, and analyze.

Now, the first step to explore the space of your mind and begin addressing the things that you regret, is to have A conversation with yourself. But keep in mind, this isn't A blame game and it definitely isn't meant for you to slip down into A rabbit hole of self-sabotage. Holding onto regret is one form of self-sabotaging, but you should move forward by identifying things that are working against you and having healthier conversations with yourself to get to the root of things. Regret is A powerful emotion, it can consume your thoughts, energy, and time. Feeling miserable is totally fine as long as you keep A check on yourself and don't let it drain you completely. No matter what your situation is, you can work on this "ghost of regret" to leave by starting doing positive things for yourself. Feed your life with passion and love, and regrets will say good-bye to you soon.

Chapter 28:

Change Your Environment For Success

Human life resembles a lot of things. Take leaves of a tree for example. Leaves change color throughout the year. Ever thought why does it happen?

Trees change the color of their leaves to adapt to the different seasons, preparing for what is coming ahead of them.

It is not exclusive only to plants. A lot of animals also have different approaches towards different climatic changes. A lot of polar birds migrate thousands of miles due South, just before the winter season comes in. A lot of fish move to warm waters in the fall season.

Ever wondered why? Because they want o make sure the survival of their species and they want to provide a habitat for their of-springs where they can flourish and nourish well.

Do you want to be a successful human being? You should make a stronger network with your species. The more you interact with your species the more you are to have a better social life, the better chances you have at learning, and the better chances of survival you have if you have someone dependable to rely on.

The effects your environment and your company have on you will determine how pessimistic, ambitious, and or organized you are. You will feel the change in the course of events just as you start to make a change in your environment.

Every man needs a productive and nourishing environment to flourish to his or her full limits. And maybe even push the limits further.

You also need to realize that whatever you are in search of will always be achievable, but you have to make a routine and a habitat where you can relax when you are feeling low.

Most of us take our health for granted. We take our sleep for granted and a disruptive sleep cycle can change our behavior. If you don't have a good place to sleep and if you don't have a nice comfortable bed or bedding to curl up in, you will not be able to restore all your creative juices.

These juices will only flow when you will let them, and for that, you need to create a window of the calming and soothing environment to sleep in.

Now if you have a goal and you know the right path to it, stay put and start by bringing in the most relevant things nearer to you. Start pushing the unnecessary thins out of your habitat and you will be forwarding one step closer to success.

We don't realize this fully but we are truly a product of our environment and our relationships.

Every new day is a new chance to bring a change in our lives. Find new things that inspire you. Find New people that motivate you. Find newer things that push you. Find better goals that make you shine bigger and better than everyone else around you.

If you are willing to change what you love the most around you, you are already far ahead on your path to success.

Chapter 29:

10 Habits of Steve Ballmer

A step to improving your business for long-term growth and profits is learning from entrepreneurs who've proven themselves the best. One case in point is Steve Ballmer, the bold, boisterous former Microsoft CEO. He left Microsoft's top management to channel his energy into owning the LA Clippers basketball club.

Ballmer is the current owner of the Los Angeles Clippers of the National Basketball Association (NBA). Forbes recently ranked him as the 11th richest person globally, with an estimated wealth of US$71.4 billion. How did he become this wealthy?

Here are 10 habits of Steve Ballmer.

1. Learn With a Purpose

Working with several school teams such as basketball and football teams and the school newspaper allowed Ballmer to develop positive energy, sociability, and assertiveness that would serve his success journey well. After graduating from Harvard, he started advertising for muffin and brownie mixes at protector and gamble. You need to seek unique and challenging experiences, anything different from your daily monotony, because it is from these experiences that you'll learn and improve.

2. Make Yourself Indispensable

Making yourself dispensable means associating well with your peers because you never know what tomorrow holds, and when they give you a chance, don't take it for granted. Ballmer's sociability and assertiveness got him close to Bill Gates during his college days, and when he needed somewhere to start his career, his friend was there. Even though he was working for his friend, he never took work for granted; instead, his dedication to work diversified Microsoft products such as the electronic game console system Xbox and the Zune family of portable media players.

3. Develop a Perspective

Sometimes your point of view creates opportunity, and other times you pick up opportunities gives you a chance to build a point of view. However, an opportunity is rarely enough without a distinctive perspective to shape a generic opportunity into something extraordinary. Ballmer challenged graduates at St. Louise to develop a point of view, just like Jack Dorsey, the co-founder of both Twitter and Square, in order to create opportunities for themselves.

4. You Can Start Small

If you want to be rich, start from somewhere, no matter how insignificant the role is. Ballmer started as an assistant to Bill Gates, where he was earning $50,000 a year. Several years later, his efforts promoted him up until he was officially named CEO, a position he stayed in until retirement. If you want to succeed in life, there is nothing wrong with starting small. Hard work, dedication, and perseverance will always get you where you want to be.

5. Don't Run Your Predecessor's Shop.

Ballmer ran Bill Gate's company until Microsoft's final reorganization but lacked Gates' unique skills. As a new executive, you have two options: change your skills to meet the organization's needs or change the organization to meet your needs. Ballmer isn't a software expert and incredibly did so well, given that he ran a company built around software expertise. Ballmer would never compete with Gates, but he did eventually make changes to Microsoft that better reflected his distinct strengths.

6. Be a Step Ahead

To ensure that application developers continued using Microsoft's DOS and that Microsoft remained ahead of their competitors, Ballmer pushed Microsoft to announce widows. He had noted a possible competition from Apple after they launched their interface model. If you want to be successful and wealthy, especially if you find yourself in a competitive business line, always be one step ahead of your competitors and be competent in the decisions you make.

7. Let your energy drive your work

Ballmer's drive to work, managerial talent, loyalty was infectious, according to his co-workers. He was friendly, easy-going with a loud, exuberant style. His high energy personality influenced a lot of business interactions, which eventually drove growth over the years and made him rich. The more boisterous you are, the easier you can convince investors.

Your attitude and energy towards work will enable you to apply your skills and gifts more effectively.

8. Numbers matter

Ballmer was a mathematician; hence you can see where his obsession for numbers is rooted from. Because today's world is data-driven, the likelihood is that his talent is more valuable now than when he was Microsoft CEO. Numbers compel you to examine the measurable facts, seek reliable information, and constantly question what is essential. According to Steve, numbers define your success and failures, hence having a solid foundation for success.

9. Keep It Brief

While many would go extra to writing a sentence to relay information, Ballmer isn't one of them; he can say what others can't in three words. Because of his accuracy, he was able to touch more people personally. When running a large organization, being wordy is the worst because, in addition to the listener losing track, you waste time, lose the point, and may cause you to say something you didn't intend to.

10. Rediscover Fun

If you no longer enjoy your job, find a way to leave. Escape the prison and find a way to reclaim the smile that everyone around you remembers so fondly. As Ballmer stepped away from Microsoft toward something that appeared to be far more enjoyable, you could also find a way to put a smile back on your face.

Conclusion

Just like Steve Ballmer, learn skills and continually work to sharpen them. Let the skills speak for you, as the better they are, the more likely opportunities will come to you.

Chapter 30:

The Lure of Wanting Luxury Items

Have you ever walked by a store and pondered over those LV bags if you were a lady? Secretly hoping that you can get your hands on one of those bags so that you can feel good about yourself when you carry them on your shoulders? Or have you ever glanced at a boutique watch shop if you were a guy hoping that you can get your hands on one of the rolexes which costs north of $10k minimum? That could be the same lust and desire for the latest and greatest cars, apple products, clothing, etc. anything you name it.

You think of saving up a year's worth of salary just to be able to afford one of these things and you see yourself feeling good about it and that you can brag to your friends and show off to people that you have the latest and most expensive product on the market. and you imagine yourself being happy that it is all you will need to stay happy.

I am here to tell you that the lure of owning luxury items can only make you happy to a certain extent. And only if purchasing these things is something of great meaning to you, like achieving a big milestone that you want to commemorate in life. In that instance, walking into that store to purchase that luxury product can be a great experience and of great significance as well. Whether it be a birthday gift to yourself, or commemorating a wedding anniversary, job/career work milestone, or any of that in nature, you will tend to hold these products with great sentimental value and hardly will you ever sell these items should the opportunity arise to make a profit from them (which is generally not the case with most things you buy).

I will argue that when you pick these products to wear from your wardrobe, you will indeed be filled with feelings of happiness, but it is not the product itself that makes you happy, but it is the story behind it, the hard work, the commemorative occasion that you will associate and remember these products for. It will transport you back in time to that place in your life when you made the purchase and you will indeed relive that emotion that took you there to the store in the first place. That to me is a meaningful luxury purchase that is not based on lust or greed, but of great significance.

But what if you are just someone who is chasing these luxury products just because everyone else has it? When you walk down the street and you see all these people carrying these products and you just tell yourself you have to have it or else? You find all the money you can dig from your savings and emergency fund to pay for that product? I would argue that in that instance, you will not be as happy as you thought you would be. These kinds of wants just simply do not carry the weight of any importance. And after feeling good for a few days after you owned that luxury good, you feel a deep sense of emptiness because it really does not make you a happier person. Instead you are someone trying to have something but with that comes a big hole in your wallet or your bank account. The enthusiasm and excitement starts to fade away and you wonder whats the next luxury good you need to buy to feel that joy again.

You see, material goods cannot fill us with love and happiness. Luxury goods are only there to serve one purpose, to reward you for your hard work and that you can comfortably purchase it without regret and worry that you are left financially in trouble. The lure of many of us is that we tend to want what we can't have. It could also turn into an obsession for many of us where we just keep buying more and more of these luxury goods to satisfy our craving for materialistic things. You will realise one day that the pursuit never ends, the more you see, the more you want. And that is just how our brains are wired.

I have a confession to make, I had an obsession for apple products myself and I always thought I wanted the latest and greatest apple products every year when a new model comes out. And every year apple seems to know how to satisfy my lust for these products and manages to make me spend thousands of dollars every time they launch something new. This addiction i would say lasted for a good 8 years until I recently realised that the excitement ALWAYS fades after a week or two. Sure it is exciting to play with it for a couple of days while your brain gets used to this incredible piece of technology sitting in front of you. But after a week or two, I am left wondering, whats next? I began to realise that what really made me happy was doing what i love, engaging in my favourite hobbies, meeting friends, and just living simply without so many wants in life. When you have less wants, you automatically go into a mindset of abundance. And that is a great feeling to have.

I challenge all of you today to question what is your real motivation behind wanted to buy luxury items. Is it to commemorate a significant achievement in your life? or is it a meaningless lust for something that you want to emulate others for. Dig deeper and you will find the answer. Thank you

Chapter 31:

10 Habits That Will Make Your Life Better

All of us desire to have better lives. We hope that someday we will have progressive and substantive lives. We should be alive to the fact that a dream without concrete plans to realize it will remain just that – a dream on paper. Our habits cumulatively bring us closer to a better life. Here are ten habits that will make your life better:

1. Honesty

Success is founded on honest work. Honesty is the backbone of a better life. To succeed, you have to be honest with yourself and other people. Doing honest work and relating with people truthfully will establish you as reliable.

Honesty is rare and when people perceive you are reliable, they will entrust you with their resources and other factors of production

2. Continuously Learning New Things

We are in a constant state of learning. It is a continuous endless process that helps us become better daily. Even the most educated people have a new life concept to learn from other people. In learning, we unlearn myths, fallacies, and misconceptions. You can improve your life by learning a new skill that will aid you to face new challenges in life. Not everything is learned in a classroom, some lessons are acquired through experience. Purpose to learn throughout your life and your life will improve.

3. Accepting Correction

Nobody is perfect. Everybody has their flaws and the earlier you identify your weaknesses and work on them, the better things will get for you. Correction does not mean that you are incompetent but rather imperfect like everybody else.

Own up to your mistakes and do not be defensive when you are corrected. The first step towards improvement is accepting your wrongs and implementing the right suggestions.

4. Boldness To Make Tough Decisions

Sometimes you need to make landmark decisions in your life. It could be severing close ties with some people or being ruthless in abandoning old retrogressive habits. A better life is guaranteed if you make the right decisions. Fortune favors the bold. Better opportunities will come when you venture into new business spaces. Although the hesitancy in trying new things is real, evaluate the possible value arising from the bold step you will take.

5. Good Socializing Habits

Making friends fast is an important life skill. It is beneficial for you to easily blend in a given setting and make friends with strangers. When you are in a new space, get to know people because they can help you navigate unfamiliar territories. Good socializing habits will protect you from attacks when new people you meet profile you as unfriendly.

6. Quick Adaptability To The Environment

Do not seek preferential treatment whenever you are in a new environment. Adapt to the prevailing conditions and you will blend well with the local population.Moreover, you can focus on other important issues when you spend little time settling down. Quick adaptability will make you live peacefully wherever life takes you.

7. Creativity

Creativity can hardly be learned formally. It is mostly acquired through experience and personal zeal. Life is a cycle with many unique challenges. You cannot tackle every challenge in the same way.
Creativity will help you come up with new ways of approaching issues. Things will work out for you when you think out of the ordinary.

8. Building Bridges

It is important not to create enmity everywhere you go because you could be unknowingly shutting doors to future opportunities. Build bridges and not walls with people you meet because the future is uncertain. Life would be easier when you do not have many enemies to worry about. Your focus would be on more important matters.

9. Consulting

Nobody has a monopoly on ideas. Seeking advice is not a sign of weakness but an appreciation that you do not know everything. You have nothing to lose and instead stand to gain a lot from the advice you get. Instead of acting blindly, consult experienced people on issues you are naïve at. Consultation is an eye-opener to many things. You can thereafter make sober decisions.

10. Complying With Authority

Every place has rules that govern the place. Law brings order and streamlines issues where there is no clarity. Seek to fulfill what is required of you wherever you are by the existing authority. It is responsible for the creation of a conducive working environment. When you comply with set rules, you contribute to your success and that of others.

In conclusion, these ten habits will make your life better. They are the existing habits of successful people. We can be like them when we follow in their steps.

Chapter 32:

Keep Working When You're Just Not Feeling It

How many times in a day do you feel like doing nothing? How many times have you had the feeling of getting exhausted and have no energy or motivation to do anything? Do you want answers to these problems? Let's analyze some things.

What were the last big achievement that made you, your family, and your friends proud? When was the last time you had this urge to do a little more work just for the sake of it? Did you feel sorry for yourself and thought how tired you are? These are the problems!

The things that don't make sense to you right now will become more meaningful and purposeful once you get out of your comfort zone. For that, you must start doing what you failed to do the last time.

These feelings of in-activeness and leisure are not a result of some circumstances but the inner voice of every human being that never sleeps and makes us feel like we cannot do this today.

More than often, a change of self is needed than a change of the scenes surrounding us. This is the major task at hand that most people fail to achieve. But we can never give up. This is in fact the spirit of living. The spirit of keep going even when the hardest times hit.

Your body should be the easiest item for you to train and get a hold of. If you are not even able to do that, then there is very little hope for you to achieve anything ever again.

So put yourself in motion and start creating. Instead of thinking about these wrong feelings that your heart gives out just to get you to sleep one more hour, use your time to get creative with life. You don't deserve a good sleep if you haven't done what was meant to be done today. You don't deserve a long breath of relaxation if you haven't tried hard enough to get out of this rut.

You don't feel like getting the job done because you still have a sense of fear and self-pity that keeps you from giving your creative energies another try.

Human beings are the summary of what they repeatedly do, so excellence can also be a habit once you make changes in your behavior for it.

If an inner voice tells you not to do something because you cannot do it, give it a trailer of what is about to come. You will get things done the very first time, and that voice will never bother you again.

These voices and feelings will make you procrastinate rather than performing those actions for real. This is no good way to use your creative energies, just to think of a beautiful scenario and not actually doing something to be in that scenario someday. And laying low because you don't feel like doing it today is the smallest hurdle to pass to get to that place.

All you need is some self-resilience and self-control and the ability to be the master of your body and I doubt there is anything that can stop you then.

Chapter 33:

10 Habits Of Happy People

Happiness is a state of joy. In happiness, one is thrilled, contented, and tickled by joy. It is often expressed through bursts of laughter amidst smiles and it cannot be hidden. Happiness is a state everyone desires but few can maintain. Here are ten habits of happy people:

1. They Are Outgoing

Happy people are very social. They easily interact with strangers and make friends faster than ordinary people. They are charming to a fault and you cannot help but love their company.

Happy people are easily noticeable in a room full of different people. They are conspicuously outgoing to initiate trips, vacations, and team-building activities. Their social nature makes them thrive both in outdoor and indoor interactions.

2. They Are Self-Driven

Happy people have a strong personality that drives them in life. They are not coerced to do something and often act out of self-will. They stand out from a population that requires much convincing before they act.

They live a purposeful life that is crystal in their minds. Happy people do not need an external influence to be happy. They genuinely derive pleasure from what they do.

3. They Wake Up Early

Happy people know the secret of waking up early and do not need persuasion to wake up earlier than everybody else.

In waking up early, they keep off conflict with other people who could ruin their day. They build the foundation of the day ahead of them in the morning and they can maintain the tempo until the end. Strangers can do very little to ruin their happiness.

4. They Are Positive About Life

Happy people are very optimistic about life. Positivity is their middle name. They hardly entertain thoughts of failure. Like all of us, happiness is a choice they have to constantly make and work towards it. It distinguishes them from everyone else.

How can you be happy if you do not see the good out of the ugly? Happy people look at the brighter side of life because the grass is not greener on the other side but where you water it.

5. They Keep The Company Of Other Happy People

Happy people keep the fire of happiness burning because they associate with like-minded people. They share ideas and strategies on how to pursue their purpose. They also encourage each other when hope is bleak.

The company of sad and angry people is devastating because it gives no room for happiness to thrive. Happy people embrace each other's company because it is all they have got if they are to stay happy.

6. They Read Success Stories

Success stories are inspiring. They make us pull our socks and give us hope to succeed as others have. Happy people read and share success stories because therein lies happiness. They bask in the glory of their friends because they believe their turn too shall come.

Happy people shun bad news and stories of despair because they are discouraging and one could succumb to depression if they are not careful.

7. They Know How To Handle Bad News And Rejection

Happy people know that rejection does not spell doom for them. They have hope that they can rise above all challenges they face and still be happy. Unlike ordinary people who take rejection personally and despair, happy people consider it as another phase of life.

Handling bad news is a skill that happy people have perfected. Although some bad news could hit them hard, they know how to soak in their happiness and not live in sadness.

8. They Are Agents Of Change

Happy people are agents of change wherever they go. They make a difference with their speech and their aura changes everything. Everybody can feel the impact of happy people wherever they are.

Happy people inspire others to be like them. They recruit others in their league of happiness because they desire to see a changing world.

9. They Are Loving And Caring

Happy people can afford to be caring because they have no traces of bitterness or anger within them. They genuinely care for the welfare of other people.

Happiness makes people loving unlike those who harbor anger. You can only give what you have and it is natural for happy people to care more and sad people hurt more.

10. They Live An Authentic Lifestyle

Authenticity is a mark of happy people. They live a genuine lifestyle without seeking to impress anyone. Their joy does not lie in the approval of strangers but the satisfaction of their needs.

Happy people live within their financial means and not in the standards that other people have put for them. Their priorities are independent of external influence.

In conclusion, happy people are easy to spot. It is everybody's dream to be happy but a very elusive one. These ten habits of happy people distinguish them from others.

Chapter 34:

10 Habits Of Happy Kids

Happy kids are unique from their peers. They are joyous throughout and it spreads even to those around them. You cannot help but love them for their charming young personality. Here are ten habits of happy kids:

1. They Love Immensely

Happy kids do not withhold their love for people who thrill them. They love deeply and it is difficult to turn them against the people they love. They always want to be carried by them and play together at the slightest opportunity.

The love of happy kids is genuine. They show their love through small acts like wanting to follow them everywhere and clinging to them when they want to leave.

2. They Easily Make Friends

Happy kids have no problem forging friendships with both their peers and adults. Their happiness attracts people to them and they get along quickly. They have a magnetic influence wherever they go.

Their loving nature coupled with a joyous attitude makes socializing with other people an easy task. Happy kids are popular in their circles for their warm friendship.

3. They Have No Sense Of Insecurity

Happy kids are not insecure. They have a sense of belonging to the family they are raised in and in the groups they belong to. They are not afraid that somebody else can replace them or that others will be favorites and overtake them.

They are self-confident and are not threatened by any competition from anybody. At their young age, it is noticeable that they promote the welfare of other children too.

4. They Are Fast Learners

Most happy kids are by default fast learners too. Although there are a few who are happy but slow learners, a majority of them quickly grasp concepts that skip the attention of unhappy kids.

Their fast learning is attributed to their positive attitude. They are eager to make things work for them and they learn fast using the most convenient method. Unlike happy kids, the unhappy ones have no interest in a majority of things happening around them making them learn associated concepts slower.

5. They Have Enough Sleep

Happy kids are not deprived of sleep. Their sleeping schedule is on time as advised by pediatricians and experienced parents. They have no insomnia that is often caused by restlessness, emotional and mental stress.

Unlike adults, kids are supposed to have a night of uninterrupted peaceful sleep for many hours. Unhappy kids have underlying factors that cause insomnia. It is a red flag that parents and guardians should address.

6. They Are Positive

Happy kids have a positive attitude towards life. They are free from stress and worry. When you pay attention to conversation among kids of the same age group, you can single out those who are happy in the manner they talk. Everything is possible to them.

Happy kids have a positive view of life and they believe that the adults in their lives can easily solve their problems. Their positivity is admirable.

7. They Are Very Creative

Happy kids are very creative. Their minds are not clogged by a lot of things and they have room to think of innovations at their age unlike their unhappy peers and adults too who are constantly worried about the source of their next provisions.

Creativity breeds in their positive attitude. They want to make life better at their level. Their innovations are simple yet a good sign of a promising kid.

8. They Explore Their Talents At A Very Young Age

Happy kids discover their passion at an early age because their happiness leads them to engage in activities they love. Parents and guardians guide them in exploring their talents and support them by buying toys for the things their children love.

Their happiness makes them enthusiastic to try new things and they eventually discover their talents. Under the right tutelage, they make very good professionals in the sectors they settle in.

9. They Eat Well

What is the connection between feeding habits and the happiness of a child? Happy kids have peace of mind that subconsciously improves their appetite.

Most stressed kids have a poor appetite because their minds are occupied with how to address the challenges they are undergoing. They eat because it's meals time and they do not want to be isolated but not because they are hungry.

10. They Have Good Health Practices

Happy kids are healthy. They are stress-free and eat well. They hardly fall sick because their immunity is not compromised. Their parents guide them in eating healthy foods and observing hygiene. This keeps diseases at bay.

Having good health contributes to their happiness because they are not in pain caused by sickness.

In conclusion, these minute habits of happy kids are mostly ignored but play a big role in their growth. Initiate them in your child and watch the transformation.

CPSIA information can be obtained
at www.ICGtesting.com
Printed in the USA
LVHW051423010222
709871LV00021B/3520